D0388900

DATE			
MAR 2 6 1992			
MAY 4 1992			
MAY 2 1 1992			
JUL 2 1 1992			
OCT 2 0 1992			
JUL 2 8 1993			
SEP 8 1993			
NOV 2 1993			

© THE BAKER & TAYLOR CO.

Rick Adelman

with

Dwight Jaynes

SIMON & SCHUSTER

NEW YORK · LONDON · TORONTO · SYDNEY · TOKYO · SINGAPORE

THE LONG, HOT WINTER

A Year in the Life of the
Portland Trail Blazers

SIMON & SCHUSTER
Simon & Schuster Building
Rockefeller Center
1230 Avenue of the Americas
New York, New York 10020

Designed by Marc Strang
Photo section designed by Caroline Cunningham

Manufactured in the United States of America

3 4 5 6 7 8 9 10

Library of Congress Cataloging in Publication Data is available

ISBN: 0-671-74852-1

The author would like to acknowledge and thank the following: My parents, L. J. and Gladys, for their constant support; my sisters and brothers, who are always there; JoAnne, Patty Monica, Clete, and Frank; Therese, Cliff, Larry, and Petey, for their acceptance and help; Gary for his guidance and input; the two Jacks—Ramsay and Mc-Mahan—each got me started in the NBA and to each I will be forever grateful; Stu Inman, who took the time to get an inexperienced community college coach started; Jim O'Connor and Roy Heideman, their early impact is not forgotten; those at Loyola-Marymount, whose encouragement gave me a chance to succeed; all my teammates, who made basketball fun and continue to support me; Dick Motta, Phil Johnson, Rolland Todd, Jack McCloskey, Scotty Robertson, and Alex Hannum, for the knowledge and help; all those at Chemeketa Community College, especially Bill Segura, Jerry Berger, Ward Paldanius, and the counseling and physical education staff; the Trail Blazer and Chemeketa players, your talents and cooperation have made me look good; Paul Allen, who took a chance and gave me an opportunity of a lifetime; Bert Kolde and the entire Blazer family, for their hard work and support; Traci Rose, John Lashway, John Christensen, and Roger Sabrowski, who are always there to help; Harry Glickman, who symbolizes the integrity and uniqueness of the Trail Blazer organization; all those associated with this special team, and Bucky Buckwalter and Brad Greenberg; John, Jack, Mike, and Dan, for their loyalty and friendship; Bob Cook, for his professionalism and timely humor; Bill Schonely, the voice of the Trail Blazers; all Trail Blazer fans throughout Oregon—you make it all worthwhile and possible; my old friend and roommate, Geoff Petrie, for his patience and wise counsel; Jerry and

Dorn, who have always been there for us; and B. B., for the beads.

—R. A.

It's always best to start at the beginning and, in my career, it was when George Pasero took a chance and hired a kid without any real experience in this business. It wouldn't have worked, though, without Bill Whitlock's help at that time. So many writers and editors, at *The Oregon Journal* and then at *The Oregonian*, have taken time to help me in the past twenty years and their names would fill another book. Thanks to them all.

I'm indebted to Terry Pluto, who assisted in the birth of this project. Jeff Neuman of Simon & Schuster immediately showed me why he's considered the best editor in the business; and his right-hand man, Stuart Gottesman, was a big help. My partner in covering the Trail Blazers, Kerry Eggers, deserves a lot of credit for his constant willingness to provide encouragement and assistance.

Most of all, though, thanks must go to the people who sacrificed most so that this book could become a reality: My family—Gail, Willie, and Beth. They've put up with the downside of a sportswriter's career—road trips, long hours, and late-night phone calls—without the fun part, getting to see the games. And they've been understanding of what the pressures of the job can sometimes bring in the way of grumpiness. Thanks gang, for everything.

—D. W. J.

October

Salem, Oregon—It's the first day of training camp and all summer long people have been warning me about what I should worry about. The big concern is that you come back after the kind of season we had last year and you're satisfied. You think you've arrived and you don't have the frame of mind that you need to be successful—that is, to win the championship.

We shocked everyone in the National Basketball Association last season by winning the Western Conference championship before losing to the Detroit Pistons in the NBA Finals. We got there so quickly. It was like we came out of nowhere; only a year before, we were swept out of the playoffs in the first round. And the big concern coming into camp is how we will respond—both to our success and to our failure, the five-game loss to the Pistons.

Sometimes, people told me, you come back and think it's going to be easy. And when that happens, all the little things—from injuries to contract problems—can tear you down.

I remember a few years back when Houston made it to

the Finals against the Celtics with Akeem Olajuwon and Ralph Sampson—the Twin Towers. They didn't win but everyone in the league rushed to copy them. It's all anyone talked about, getting two big men to match up with them. It was the coming thing. But they had one brief year and it all came down around their ears. I worry about that a little bit.

In some ways, it's only after you lose in the Finals that you realize you had a chance to win. It was really discouraging to get that far and lose, but there was a sense of satisfaction, too. We made it all the way to the Finals in what was really our first season together as a team. Nothing like that was expected of us.

I moved our training camp out of the Portland area last year, to the state capital forty-five minutes down Interstate 5 south of Memorial Coliseum. I wanted a change of atmosphere and we found it at Willamette University, where we had an outstanding training camp. The city of Salem is special to me; it's where I started my coaching career at Chemeketa Community College.

We have pretty much the same team we had in the Finals last June—only better.

Terry Porter, who we feel is an emerging superstar, is back at point guard. Clyde Drexler, who is already a superstar, is our off-guard. We have Buck Williams, a first-team all-defensive player, at power forward, and Jerome Kersey, one of the league's most underrated and hardest-working players, at small forward. At center, Kevin Duckworth has already played in an all-star game and is one of our main offensive threats.

We open camp with a logjam behind Drexler at the 2-guard. We added Danny Ainge, a former Oregon high school star, in a trade that cost us a couple of future draft picks and Byron Irvin, a rookie guard who didn't play much last season. We also have Drazen Petrovic, the popular second-year player from Yugoslavia, at that spot.

At the point, Danny Young is Porter's backup—a steady but unspectacular player who is a good defender and clutch

3-point shooter. We also have Shaun McDaniel, a five-foot-eight scrapper who performed well in our summer league, in camp to battle Young for a job; it's probably one of only two personnel questions of any consequence in camp. We want to give McDaniel, who showed the ability in the summer league to go downcourt and pick people's pockets defensively, a chance.

The other big question mark in training camp is our only rookie, six-foot-ten Alaa Abdelnaby out of Duke. He didn't play well in our summer program, and we'll be taking a hard look at him during the exhibition season. Alaa has very good footwork and is fundamentally sound on offense. He has a lot of offensive potential. We want to see if he can help us, but we have three quality players returning as backups to our starters up front so there aren't a lot of minutes available. We have Mark Bryant backing up Williams at power forward and Cliff Robinson, who had an outstanding rookie season last year, coming off the bench at all three spots up front. Reliable veteran Wayne Cooper is our backup center.

I made a point of talking with our starters prior to camp. Just like all the writers, fans, and well-wishers who approached me about it all summer, I wanted to know how they were taking the loss in the Finals. I was glad to see that they all seemed to have a very good mental approach to training camp. They weren't too caught up in what we had done last year. They were more disappointed than satisfied, and I liked that. But we have one big problem coming into camp that worried me a lot.

Promises were made last season that the contracts for Clyde, Jerome, and Buck would be redone during the off-season. As we opened camp, none of them had been—which, by the way, is normal. There's always a lot of jockeying around during the summer, and then just before training camp it finally gets serious. Still, I'm worried about how those three players are going to react if it drags on through training camp. I'm trying not to think about what might happen if these contracts don't get redone.

You have to understand the business from the players' point of view. They have to do what they can, when they can, and when the opportunity presents itself. But you have the rest of the team to deal with, too. It's a real tough situation.

But all three players showed up on the first day of camp and the contract side of it never showed up on the floor at all. As a team, we didn't talk about it; we just went about our business. Geoff Petrie, our senior vice president/operations, is in charge of the contract negotiations, and he'll keep me informed about them all along.

I felt going into camp that by adding Danny Ainge and subtracting Byron Irvin, who didn't play a lot, we had helped ourselves without paying too steep a price. Danny has great experience; he's been on a winner, he's been a scorer, and he's come off the bench. Plus his personality is different from that of anyone else we had on our team. He's a guy who will say what's on his mind—to anyone. He always has an opinion and isn't shy about expressing it. Most of our players are very reserved off the court. Danny isn't. I thought his addition, combined with the further development of Cliff, would give us two guys who could come in off the bench and really hurt the other team. That's something we were missing all last season; we had dry spells that hurt us all year, including the Finals.

I didn't think I needed to approach the team on the first day with a huge "Get one for the Gipper" speech. My talk the first day consisted mostly of restating what we had done the previous year. We shocked the league by what we did. We came together so quickly. We had added some pieces and we think Danny Ainge can help us. If we really have arrived, it's time to go out and show it. Our practice, I told them, had to show that we were serious about what we were doing and not complacent.

I was pleased because we had a good practice. Ainge seemed to fit in right from the start. Everybody competed hard. I suspected, even though our off-season was so short—less than four months—that our players were ready; during our physicals, most of them showed up in the best shape they'd ever been in. I could tell right from the start there was no complacency on our team. If anything, there was more resolve that we were going to play harder this year than we did last year.

We practice only once a day during training camp, probably one of the few teams in the NBA that doesn't go through several days of "daily doubles"—two practices a day. That came from Mike Schuler, the man I replaced as Trail Blazer head coach. Mike got the reputation here for being tough and rigid, but he wasn't as unwilling to change as a lot of people thought. He came up with the idea that instead of two two-hour practices a day, why not just have one three-hour session? I remember him saying, "Let's see if we can accomplish the same things in three hours." I think it's the best way to run your camp.

First, you usually have some veteran players, who are also usually your best players, sitting out the morning practice to rest aching muscles or minor injuries. So you don't get much accomplished because you don't have your veteran guys going through the morning drills, or if you do, they're going through them at half speed.

Second, and this really does matter, the players love it. It gives guys the whole day to recover from the previous day's practice, and they're more ready to go hard. They practice harder. We've had fewer people sitting out of practices. I think once we got used to the three-hour practices, we got every bit as much accomplished in them as we did in two two-hour practices.

I plan to stick to it. I think I would change only if I had a really young team where I had to work a lot on individual things and accomplish a lot. Then I would probably go back to two-a-days. But for a team such as ours, it's an ideal setup. I know I would have loved it as a player.

I believe starting this camp that we are as good as any team in the league. I think we finally have an identity, the way the really good teams do. And I think the players believe in their identity.

Our fans, of course, have already been thinking ahead to a championship. The attitude in our state, where the Blazers are the center of all sports attention, is that anything less than a championship this season will be a failure. Expectations are high—and with good reason. The trip to the Finals set a high standard for us.

Some people say Detroit beat us last year by getting under our skin. People say that Bill Laimbeer disrupted us. Frankly, I think Isiah Thomas had a lot more to do with beating us than Laimbeer did. I think Laimbeer's contribution was overblown. It was media hype. Isiah Thomas making clutch shots is what beat us. And we have to put it behind us now and start again.

I think our team came to camp knowing its identity is as a team that hits the boards, plays good defense, and plays hard. Buck Williams has given us an interior defensive identity that we never had before and that we had to have in order to be a great team. And he helped make us the best rebounding team in the league. Those are the areas where it takes consistent hard work to be great.

Prior to last year, we were always a talented team, but we never had that identity. I think you have to form that in order to win. We built it last season and it was a given from Day One of training camp this year.

Terry, Buck, Jerome, Clyde . . . they set the tone right there on the first day. In previous years we had some guys who just went out and practiced, with no real purpose. Well, it's not that way anymore. We know who we are.

We defend, we rebound, and we play hard. And we know that when we do that, we stay in games. And we know the other teams know it. They know we're going to be tough. They know we know we're going to win. Knowing that makes it easier to dig down and work harder. It's a very satisfying cycle for a coach to see.

October 7, 1990

Salem—Our concentration continues to be good, even though there isn't a lot of progress on those new contracts. This camp is different from most because no jobs are at stake. Everyone is on a guaranteed contract. It was not that way for me as a player.

Not a lot of people knew who I was when I was drafted in the seventh round by San Diego in 1968. I really never thought I had a chance of playing in the NBA. But I made the team, and after breaking my jaw during the exhibition season, I played the first two and a half months of my professional career with a hockey mask over my face.

I never really thought I'd ever get the chance to coach the Portland Trail Blazers, either. I didn't have a high profile while I was an assistant coach with the team.

If you're a good assistant in this league, only one or two other people in the organization are apt to know about you, unless you've been a major-college head coach. But unless the general manager takes the time to talk with you—and then only if you feel comfortable relaying your true feelings to him—nobody but the head coach is going to know you.

Even a head coach cannot possibly know how good one of his assistants would be with his own team. I heard Jack Ramsay say it many times—no one knows how good even the best assistant coach would be as a head coach until he gets his own team.

A good assistant doesn't bad-mouth what's going on with the team and won't betray the head coach. It's the head coach's team. A good head coach will talk with you about your ideas, but the final decisions are his, and your job is to go along with them.

A good assistant is in a unique situation. The best quality he can have is loyalty to the head coach. Within the meetings of the coaching staff, everyone gives his opinion on all phases of the game—from style of play to his feelings about players. It is vital for the head coach to hear the opinions of his assistants. In meetings of the entire team hierarchy, an assistant won't talk as much, and will defer to the head coach, unless directly addressed. Most questions are asked of the head man—not his assistants.

There are some situations where you see assistant coaches sitting around the pressroom before a game talking to the media, other coaches, or general managers. Many are doing it to let people get to know them—or are promoting themselves. If the team's situation is rough, they can put themselves in a precarious situation, which could lead to second-guessing the head coach.

The real truth of the matter is that no one really knows what style a guy will use until he gets his own team. And you never know how he'll handle situations until they happen.

I know Atlanta coach Bobby Weiss well and played with him at Chicago under Dick Motta. I would have bet money that Bobby, who was an assistant to Dick for years, would have run a system similar to Dick's. But he got to San Antonio and ran a passing game totally different from Dick's system. I would have sworn he wouldn't have done that. But Bob's intelligent and knows what kind of game he likes, and he did it his own way.

But I never thought I'd have that chance. It was a long road and a lot of that time it was as if I were still wearing the mask.

I finished up playing professional basketball in 1975. About that time I realized that while I was playing ball and finishing up my schooling, guys had been out there and now had a ten-year head start on me in the job market. So I was behind all those people and it was difficult.

Even though I had a master's degree in history, I couldn't get a job and had to return to school to get my secondary-teaching credential. I hadn't made a lot of money in the league.

Weiss, a former teammate of mine in Chicago, owned a restaurant-bar in Santa Ana, California, and I helped out the manager by tending bar for him and closing the place while I was getting my teaching credential. Though interesting, it was no lifestyle. You work nights and it got pretty depressing. It wasn't quite like Cheers. "Coach" wasn't there. Norm never showed up. It was a lot darker place, too. But at the time I needed money, and no teaching jobs were available. From Phil Vukicevich, who coached the University of San Francisco when I was playing at Loyola, I heard about a job with Converse. He was their sales and promotional representative in southern California and was going to be transferred to northern California. Dick Garibaldi, who was coaching at Santa Clara when I was in college, was the regional manager at that time, so I knew a lot of people working for them.

The job was a lifesaver at the time because I couldn't get one coaching or teaching. We were living in Costa Mesa, in Orange County, and so we wouldn't have to move. It was great because I was still somewhat involved in basketball. I had Orange County all the way to San Diego and everything east to Phoenix—a huge territory. And athletic shoes in southern California were a big thing.

At that time, though, we were talking about nothing but canvas shoes, the Chuck Taylor All-Stars. Converse had a few running shoes, but they weren't high quality. They had just started selling leather basketball shoes, but had lots of problems with them at the time. Given the competition, they were a tough sell.

The Chuck Taylors were great. Everybody still wanted those. But I worked on commission and didn't make a lot off those. They were fairly inexpensive even then. It made for a tough job with a lot of driving.

I was responsible for the Phoenix Suns, too, and that was a real pain. The company had just come out with their leather shoes, and everyone wanted them in colors and you had to get them to the teams on time, and then when the shoes got there, they ripped out all the time and you had to replace them. You always had that headache.

Ronnie Lee, the great collegiate star from the University of Oregon, was with the Suns then and he wore our shoe. He was my biggest worry. I never saw a player put so much stress on a pair of shoes. Everything the guy did was all-out. He put his heart into every cut, every drive, and every defensive possession.

Unfortunately for me, he wound up ripping our shoes about every other day. Converse had some great people and they worked hard on the problems, but it took time to iron them out. Ronnie Lee put those shoes to a stiff test.

I found out quickly that I didn't really enjoy selling, at least not that type of selling. But I was very appreciative at the time because I needed the job, and it was definitely better than tending bar.

After a year, Converse said to go ahead and take a vacation, and we went back up to Oregon to see some of our old friends and be godparents for Geoff Petrie's son, Michael, who was being baptized. Larry Steele, a good friend of mine and a former teammate with the Trail Blazers, called and said that Ted Wilson, the NAIA Hall of Fame coach at Linfield College, had told him they were looking for a coach at Chemeketa Community College in Salem. I knew nothing about junior colleges in Oregon, but I called the athletic director and told him I was interested in talking to them if they were interested in me.

I didn't realize that they had closed the applications and it wasn't really basketball coaching. The job, just created in the counseling department, called for an "articulation specialist." This person was to be the liaison between the high schools in the area and the junior college, trying to recruit more high school graduates to the junior-college system. The basketball job was just a part of it. They kind of explained the position to me, but I decided to do a little research of my own. My brother Clete knew a guy at Long Beach City College and they had someone there in a similar position. I talked to the guy and he explained what he did and gave me some information.

I came up to Oregon, went into the interview room, and there were four or five counselors. I knew immediately they were not happy with my being there because they had apparently already closed out the interview process and had decided on three finalists. They had kind of been forced to interview me because Ward Paldanius, the athletic director at the time, wanted me for the basketball job—which didn't really have a lot of weight at the time.

The interview proved interesting. Initially they weren't real happy, but I could tell right away that having done what I did at Long Beach really helped. Once they asked me a few questions, they realized I had done some research and I think it changed their minds about me. I left, though, and didn't have a whole lot of hope.

Much to my surprise, they called me back and offered me the job. My wife, Mary Kay, and I had to decide whether to take it while we were driving back to California. Obviously we decided to do it. We just picked up and moved to Oregon in 1977—both of us leaving our families behind. Though a major move at the time, it was the best thing we ever did.

I'll always be grateful to those people at Chemeketa— Ward, Jerry Berger, and Bill Segura. I think the experience I got at Chemeketa influenced me an awful lot. Working in the counseling department taught me the value of listening. It really helps when you listen and think before you react, as a coach or as anything in life.

What happens in the NBA—or anywhere at the pinnacle of your profession—is that you start to think you know everything. One must never look at other people and be closed-minded to their ideas. You may not think they know as much as you do, but that doesn't mean what they say isn't valid. Once you think you know it all, you close yourself off to good ideas, but what's worse is that when people realize you're not listening to them, they'll stop listening to you. Then you might as well know nothing at all. That's when the communication dies.

Believe me, there are a lot of worse places to get your training to be an NBA coach than the counseling department of a junior college. The things I learned there might be the most important lessons I ever learned.

October 9, 1990

Salem—One of the biggest concerns of training camp is getting through it without major injuries to key players. So far we're doing fine. Everything is going great, and the people at Willamette are doing an excellent job of making us feel at home. It's certainly a much better facility than we had when I was coaching at Chemeketa.

We had to play in the old Salem Armory because we had no gym at the school and not even any physical education facilities. The floor was hard and it stank in there. It wasn't a good place to recruit to, and they didn't really want you to do any recruiting, anyway, since basketball was not a high priority and they had never done real well. It was a low-profile; there wasn't a lot of pressure to win and you were left alone.

I found out right away that the toughest part of the job was to convince kids in Oregon it was okay to go to a junior college. That was totally foreign to me because in California, junior college was a viable option. If you didn't get a scholarship, or sometimes even if you did, you went to a junior college to begin with—because it was free. It wasn't a put-down or anything.

In Oregon people looked at junior colleges as such a put-down. In Oregon, you didn't go to JCs, you went to small colleges.

It's too bad more high school graduates don't realize that community colleges offer the same required classes for the freshman and sophomore years, at tremendous savings. Community college is an option that's too often overlooked by young men and women—whether they're athletes or not.

The thing was, though, I was always fairly good friends with a lot of the high school coaches in Oregon, and since I was just a guy starting out, I was just trying to learn how to coach and I made sure I didn't approach them with the attitude that I knew everything—because I certainly didn't. I went to the camps in the area and tried to learn, and I talked to them about our program at Chemeketa.

I tried to see as many high school games as I could, and I tried to recruit kids from solid high school programs coached by men like Barry Adams, Nick Robertson, Ken Harris, and Bob Cantonwine. It was important for them to have a solid background because in junior college you don't have a lot of time. You don't have four years with these guys; you have to bring them together quickly, so I wanted guys who were fundamentally sound.

We began to get a lot of very good kids from Oregon. And I felt you could win with those kids, if you got the good ones who weren't quite being recruited by Division I schools but wanted a chance to show what they could do. Once I knew whom to look for, it got easier to recruit.

My last year there we had the best team we'd ever had. We went to the regional at Southern Idaho and beat the host team, winning the regional title—the first and only Oregon community college men's basketball team to do that. But there was a budget crunch at the school that year—there was a budget crunch every year—and they said there would be no travel to national tournaments and that we couldn't go on. Obviously, our kids wanted to go. Money was left over from the regional tournament for travel, and I had people lined up in Salem who would have backed us. It wouldn't have cost the school a cent, but they still wouldn't let us go. It was purely political, and very disheartening.

I realized then that I had to make a decision. To get a head-coaching job at a Division I school, you have to either go there first as an assistant or go to a national tournament and do well. Since the latter wasn't going to be an option for me, I had to think about either taking an assistant's job at a big school or just accept the fact of where I was and be satisfied with it.

I just thought, I'll stay at Chemeketa and be content with what I have. I enjoyed the students and the players I worked with and the staff. It was a good job in a nice area of Oregon.

Two years earlier, however, I had interviewed with Portland coach Jack Ramsay. I wasn't sure if I should call him then because I didn't really know him, but I did, then went up and talked to him. He told me he had someone else in mind.

Now, in the spring of 1983, I was teaching a racquetball class when someone came in and told me I had a phone call. I told them to take a message, but they said it's Jack Ramsay and he needs to talk to you. I said, Jack Ramsay?

I went to the phone and he told me that Jimmy Lynam, his assistant coach at the time, had taken the Clipper job and asked me if I had any interest in being his assistant. It was just the right time because we had just been told we couldn't go to the national tournament. Boy, did I have an interest.

He said, okay, I need to talk to you right away. I went into Portland the next day and talked to him for about forty-five minutes at the most. We didn't really talk about anything. He just asked me about my philosophy and how my team played—he was just kind of feeling me out.

My philosophy then was much as it is now: I always try to run. You have to adapt to the talent you have, but you always try to run because that's the most fun way to play. Players like it the best. I've always felt you need some kind of structure in what you do; you can't just totally free-lance. That's what we did at Chemeketa and what we do now. We run and we vary our structure according to the talent we have—the more talent, the less structure.

I don't like to be trapped in one particular style. I think you have to encourage your players, even at the junior-college level, to be creative. Your better players need that. Usually when you have a little bit of structure and you demand certain things, your players will follow the rules and begin to form roles for themselves. That's much better than when you impose a complete patterned style on them; they learn what they can do, but they don't feel so restricted. When they do that, you can get them to better understand their strengths. Even in the passing game—the free-form offense we use with the Trail Blazers—people have certain strengths, certain positions, and certain responsibilities. When the players understand that, your better players end up with the ball in the spots on the floor where they can best take advantage.

The danger of this is that it's not as consistent as an offense for a more patterned team. You're going to make more mistakes and have some periods where you don't do well. But if you do it right, you're going to have spurts where you do very well and blow games open.

With the Trail Blazers we have so many great athletes who are very similar in the way they play. They're slashers and they're creative. They can get to the basket. They go to the boards. They're active people. Those things have become our strengths as a team.

We're a good rebounding team. We're a hardworking team. There's a purpose and a mental toughness about the way we play. But we have weaknesses, too. We're not a great shooting team. We don't have a lot of patience in our offense sometimes. We don't have a great post-up player who can get us points by just isolating and shooting over his man—the way James Worthy or Kevin McHale does. Our components aren't based on that.

That's why we use the passing game. Our people can be active and slash without the defense locking in on them. When we struggle, it's usually because we haven't been together that long. We have dry spells because we don't show patience and we shoot the ball before we've moved the defense around enough to create opportunities.

But unless I had the kind of athletes I have with the Blazers, I don't think I would be as unrestrictive as I am now. You have to play the way your personnel dictates you can play.

Ramsay told me he'd call me back the next day and I went home. I told my wife that I didn't know what he was thinking. It wasn't much of an interview. I figured we might as well forget it. But he called me back the next morning and we talked for about two and a half hours on the phone. He was leaving for New York that night for the league meetings and said he wanted to make his decision that afternoon.

He asked me a lot of questions about basketball and my

philosophy. Little did I know that after I left Portland he called I don't know how many people around the league. He called a lot of people who knew me. He was doing his research. He told me after our long chat on the phone that he had one other candidate whom he had to talk to, which was George Karl, who was later an NBA head coach at Cleveland and Golden State.

Ramsay told me he'd get back to me no later than four o'clock that afternoon. So we just sat around the rest of the day waiting for that telephone call.

But no call came in.

We waited and waited. Finally, I went upstairs and discovered that one of the kids had left the phone off the hook for about an hour. I put it back on and thought, you've got to be kidding. I knew he was leaving that night for New York. But he called me back about four-thirty and said, it's your job if you want it.

It was amazing. In three days our whole world had changed, but I was ready. I talked to Mary Kay and we just felt it was the right time. And I remember thinking at the time—worrying a little about security—that if you were going to take an assistant's job under anybody in the NBA, Jack was about as secure as you could get. He was just so respected.

I found out a lot about security later. I remember talking to Blazer president Harry Glickman and trying to get a contract longer than a single season. I felt if Jack had a three-year contract and wanted me as his assistant, then I should have the same number of years on my contract. Harry said not to worry about it, that the only way Jack wouldn't be coaching the team would be if he died.

Well, in 1986 the Trail Blazers changed coaches and Jack is still alive and feeling great.

But how could I not take the job as his assistant? Jumping from junior college to the NBA and working for one of the most respected coaches in the league? It's funny how you get jobs. I talked to him one time and happened to run into him again, and it stuck in his mind. I think he liked the fact that I had played and then gone back and got experience coaching in college.

I got lucky. The timing was perfect. I had pretty much reconciled myself to coaching at small colleges the rest of my life.

October 10, 1990

Portland—We practiced in Salem in the morning, then broke camp and headed to Portland. The players had some time to get resettled, then were to meet at the airport for a bus ride to Seattle.

The plan was to bus to Seattle so we could catch an early flight the next morning for Honolulu, the site of our first exhibition game, October 12, against the Lakers. We would be flying back into Portland after the two games at Honolulu, so we wanted our cars at the airport.

That was a great plan except that when we left Salem I had no idea whether I would be seeing Clyde Drexler or Buck Williams for a few days. They still hadn't reached agreement on new contracts, and each let it slip to the media in the morning that they were thinking about not making the first trip as a way to force the issue a little bit.

I know from being a player myself that they have strong feelings about what they think they deserve and what they've done for the team. But I'm also working for the organization. Down deep, I don't think it would be disastrous if they missed the two games in Hawaii. But I want them there.

I know Geoff is still working hard at getting it done and he told me that he was making progress. I'm not in the dark on it. I honestly feel it's going to get done. And as much as I want to open the exhibition season with all of our players, I think the worst thing I could do is be distraught or act as if the world is coming to an end. We have eight exhibition games. We're a pretty solid group. I'm not going to panic if two guys don't show up, because I'm sure the issue will soon be settled.

I stopped at the airport gas station this afternoon on the way to catch the bus, and there was Buck. I felt good right then, because it was obvious he had decided to make the trip. But I still didn't know if Clyde was going. But then I drove into the parking lot, found the bus, and when I got on, Clyde was already there.

I really felt good. The players had shown that they wanted us to get off to a good start, and when I saw them there, I felt they'd really made a commitment. I think everyone on the team realized that. It also showed a lot of faith in our ownership, having the confidence that things would be worked out fairly.

That kind of trust is so important. We're all trying to go down the same road, and what could have been such a disruptive situation wasn't.

October 11, 1990

Honolulu—We practiced at a local high school and it went okay, but I have to confess I wasn't enamored of the two-game trip to Hawaii because you lose some days of practice. Had we been scheduled for only six exhibition games, I wouldn't have minded so much, but we need practice time and we're playing a full slate of eight exhibition games— two too many in my opinion.

We need to work on our halfcourt game, and practice, not games, is the way to do that. The Lakers had their whole camp there, so it was different for them. But our trip is so rushed and I would rather be at home practicing. People think, oh, wow, you're going to Hawaii. But this isn't the time of year to be going on vacation. We're supposed to be going to work.

We play the Lakers tomorrow night, and Clyde reached agreement on his contract extension today. When I heard that, I felt immediate relief. Now that his is done, Buck's will be done next, then Jerome's. I think everything is going to work out fine.

Geoff and the coaching staff went out and had a relaxing dinner near Waikiki and things looked pretty good. We're looking forward to the games against the Lakers, to see how far along we are as a team and to get our first look at them under their new coach, Mike Dunleavy—who was hired seemingly from out of nowhere to replace Pat Riley.

When Mike Schuler became the Portland head coach in 1986, I didn't even get an interview for the job. I was told then that the club didn't even want to keep me on the staff because I was considered a clone of Jack Ramsay's. They wanted to wipe the slate clean.

Well, I may have learned a lot from Jack, but I wasn't Jack's clone.

But that's the perception people had because I was loyal to Jack, even when things got bad and others in our organization were doing everything they could to divorce themselves from him. This happens a lot when a team is struggling. No one knows how to act around a coach when his team is not winning.

When I came in, I was his personal pick as his assistant. I was quiet and new to the league. I had coached my own team at a community college, but hadn't even been an assistant in the NBA. I didn't really even know what the job entailed.

I didn't say a lot at meetings and not a lot was asked of me. I listened a lot. If someone asked me a question about Jack, I was not going to talk about him or say, well, yes, we should be able to do this better. I respected him so much, I know he knew more than I did. He's probably forgotten more about this game than I've ever learned.

Jack did a lot of things that I didn't necessarily agree with, but he made the decisions. It was his team. He was such a strong personality that he always knew what he wanted to do. And he had been very successful.

Basically I was the only assistant coach around the team. Bucky Buckwalter was an assistant, but his job was to scout college talent after training camp, so he wasn't around much of the season. I was pretty much on my own, but my main job was to prepare for the opponents—to get the scouting reports ready.

Jack had been in the league so long. He was amazing. He could look at videotapes for half an hour or forty minutes and say, well, okay, they're running this play and we'll just defend it this way. That's the way he was—a confident person who knew what he wanted to do.

I think some people in our organization thought I was a yes-man who didn't have much to say. Then when things started to go a little south on Jack, I think I got a bit of an attitude about the way people perceived him. All of a sudden people thought he wasn't a good coach and that he couldn't communicate. I thought that was all baloney. He knew what he was doing.

Once they decided to let him go, it was as if I weren't even there.

I was glad Mike kept me on the staff because I didn't want to move our family. We love Portland. But the club didn't even talk to me when they let Jack go. I was just out there and my future hinged on whether or not Mike wanted to keep me. They wanted to start fresh, which meant some people thought Mike shouldn't keep me.

I think the only reason I wasn't let go immediately was that Glickman spoke up on my behalf. But I went several weeks after Mike was named head coach without knowing what was going on.

I think the big reason Mike kept me on the staff was that people in the league spoke up on my behalf. People from the late Jack McMahon—my first coach—to Jerry West to Don Nelson encouraged him to keep me. I've got to give Mike a tremendous amount of credit because people were telling Mike he shouldn't keep me, but he still did. That says a lot about Mike.

My role under Mike changed somewhat. We had two assistants—myself and Jack Schalow. Things were much more intense than under Jack, I think because it was Mike's first head-coaching job. He had been an assistant at New

Jersey and Milwaukee. Jack paid attention to detail, but detail was extremely important to Mike.

Mike's philosophy was that we could do everything possible to make sure no stone was unturned. I was still in charge of scouting opponents, but it became much more extensive under Mike. Where Jack would want to look at videotape of an opponent's previous game, Mike wanted to see two or three games to make sure we had everything completely covered. Jack might look at a quarter of a game with me. Mike would look at the whole game, then we would go over it again. I think that came from Mike's training in Milwaukee under Don Nelson; Nellie wanted that detail, so did Mike.

Though it was a lot different for me, it also helped me. It made me more organized because you had to be extremely organized or you would fall behind. One way that Jack and Mike were alike was that neither one wanted me to go out and scout teams in person very often. They both felt we could get whatever we needed off tapes, and they wanted me around with the team. I'm the same way now. We don't send our assistants out too often to look at opponents, except at the very start of the season or before the playoffs.

I'm fortunate to have two outstanding men as my assistant coaches. Jack Schalow works with our big guys, and John Wetzel works with the other guys during practice. When we scrimmage, I give them each a team and I try to oversee.

John does the pregame scouting of our opponents and gets help from Jack early in the season. Once the season is under way, Jack concentrates on our postplay and the evaluations of our own team. When we play a team again, Jack knows what worked for us and what didn't. Then John shows us what that team has been doing recently. When you get right down to it, John does the pregame stuff and Jack does the postgame stuff.

For what John Wetzel does, you can't find a better person in this league. He has had tremendous experience. He was an assistant for years to one of the best coaches in the league, John MacLeod. Then he finally got a shot at being a head coach at Phoenix and it was awful. He never had a chance from day one: they made major trades and had a drug scandal. It was ridiculous. John is really knowledgeable and gets along well with our players. Anyone who would judge him by the year in Phoenix is nuts.

Mike brought him in and then suddenly Mike was gone. He's kind of run the gamut in this league. He was in a comfortable situation, a longtime assistant to a successful head coach. Then he had a job torn out from under him after just one season as a head coach. Then he came here with someone who was successful, and then suddenly, the man who brought him in was gone. He must have been nervous about that, but I've found his experience is invaluable and he really knows the league. There's no doubt he should be a head coach again, and I just know he will. He's paid his dues and been successful. I think if we continue to do well here, it will eventually provide him another opportunity to be a head coach.

Jack Schalow is a lot different from John. Jack has done it all. He's been a successful college head coach at Seattle University, been an assistant at several good college programs, and was a head coach in the CBA who had his team playing for the championship. Mike hired him, and at that time he was still basically a scout. He had gotten away from the coaching end of it, but now I think he's really back into coaching. He really seems to be enjoying it again.

The thing about Jack is he gets along so well with the players. He's so knowledgeable and he teaches so well. He has a great feel for keeping a guy up or getting a guy going. Jack will also someday, I believe, get a chance to be a head coach. He has all the experience and has been successful on every level.

I've never made John or Jack a "number one assistant." I think that's a real crock in this league, the idea that one guy is the number one guy and the other is something less. They're assistant coaches. They get along well together and get along with our players. I can't ask for more experience at all kinds of different levels, and as far as their quality as people, you couldn't ask for more. I just never worry with them. They're so solid and loyal, but candid with me in their input. They make my job much easier.

The funny thing is, when Mike came in, I was immediately perceived as being in *his* corner. Pretty soon, I became Mike Schuler's clone rather than Jack Ramsay's clone. Larry Weinberg, who owned the team when I first joined the organization, wrote me a nice letter recently and congratulated me on our success and said he just didn't know me at the time Mike was hired. He didn't know anything about me.

I understand that. It wasn't his job to get to know the assistant coaches, and no one else bothered. But he's right; he didn't know me.

The nature of this business is that everyone is trying to protect his job and his little kingdom. It's no different from any other job I've ever been around, from coaching in junior college to selling shoes for Converse. Everyone is always trying to protect his spot. You just have to accept that. And that's why I thought the next time they hired a coach they were going to hire some big name who had proved himself somewhere else.

When things began to go bad for Mike, I never thought for a moment I would get the job. The only way I was going to get it was the way I got it—with the word *interim* in front of the title.

Assistants usually get head jobs in one of two ways. Either a general manager takes a liking to you—as Jerry West did with Dunleavy—and gives you your chance, or you go around the league and basically apply for jobs. You have to run for office. You eat dinner in the pressroom every night, get to know the right people, and pretty soon, every time there's a coaching vacancy your name pops up. Suddenly, you're a candidate and you get a chance.

But I couldn't do it that way. I never had time for that. The only way I was going to get a job was the way I got it. When Mike was fired on February 18, 1988, I was given the job of finishing the season. It wasn't the best of circumstances. I didn't feel good about taking the job under those conditions.

They offered it to me and told me I had to take the job

under certain conditions: first, Wetzel was going to be sent out scouting. I don't know why, except that I guess he was perceived as being too close to Mike. And second, Schalow was going to be my defensive coordinator—or something like that. I had no problem with that. Jack and I got along well and he is still with me. All of this sounded good, but it really didn't make very much sense.

I had no recourse about this, but I brought John back as soon as I could because I needed both him and Jack. I had only until the end of the season to show what I could do. There were all kinds of problems and it was really going to be tough. But I've always believed that it isn't as much the opportunities you get but what you do with them when you get them. I had my chance and I wanted to do everything I could with it.

Mike was so intense as a coach and as a person. All he ever wanted to do was the best job he could of coaching the Trail Blazers. It was his life. Coaching was his one ambition in life from the time he was a little kid. He worked his way up, by working hard.

Everybody is different and what you do has to fit your personality. Mike's intense desire to succeed is evident in the way he approaches practice, game preparation—everything. There's nothing wrong with that. It's his personality; it works for him. He's not as intense as he is portrayed in the media, but once you are labeled as being a certain way, it's difficult to change that perception.

I think I'm quite the opposite of Mike, probably because our backgrounds are so totally different. He worked hard to get to the top of his profession. I played professionally, went back to school, got a job at a junior college, and then suddenly, out of nowhere, I was given a job as an assistant with the Trail Blazers.

I approach a lot of things differently from Mike. If I fail at this job, I think I would be just as disappointed but not as devastated as Mike was.

I don't think his personality was the reason he was fired as coach of the Portland Trail Blazers. I just think that when you become a head coach, you can't prepare yourself for and can't be taught how to handle a lot of problems. There are pressures and things demanded of you that I didn't know about until I got the job. A lot of things are going on behind the scenes.

With Mike, the biggest problem was with Kiki Vandeweghe. Kiki was our starting small forward, but Jerome Kersey was coming on and bidding for a starting job. Then Kiki suffered his back injury in the summer prior to Mike's final season. There was friction because Kiki couldn't play during training camp, and in fact, he was told he could stay at home and not even come to camp.

Steve Johnson had a great season under Mike, but injuries began to catch up with him and it got to the point that he could hardly ever practice. There were some contract problems and the team changed ownership. The people who had hired Mike were no longer around.

We almost became prisoners of our own success because in Mike's first two seasons we had probably overachieved a little. That created expectations that we were going to make a run at the Lakers, which we really weren't good enough to do, with the personnel Mike had. We had definite holes in our team.

Pretty soon, because of several of these problems working in concert, some of our players became more concerned with their individual circumstances than with whether we were winning or losing. When that happens, everyone starts lining up and taking sides, and the coach can't do a whole lot about that, other than change personnel.

Mike was trying, but there wasn't much he could do. No matter what you do you're going to alienate someone. Pretty soon people are saying the coach has lost control of the team. And you have, because the situation is one that can't be controlled.

I still say, and I was involved in the meetings with our management people, that everyone in our organization was aware of the problems we had on the team. Everybody knew Steve Johnson was hurting. He wasn't the same player he had been before. And everyone knew Kiki was gone. He was in L.A. because of his injury and Mike had no control over that.

But all of these things created a kind of constant murmur around the team. You have it at practice and you have it at games. Then you lose a few games and the volume goes up. The complaints get louder and the frustration grows.

We just had no idea what to do. We talked—Mike, Geoff Petrie, John, and I—for hours about how to right the situation. We needed to change personnel, but it was the middle of the season and we were stuck with what we had. Soon, it was the old sports cliché at work: it's easier to change one guy, the coach, than it is to change twelve players.

People look back and say Mike was too intense for our team. Well, Mike was intense. But during his first two seasons in Portland we were very successful, he was named coach of the year, and no one was saying he was too intense.

I think it's possible over time for a coach to wear thin. It might have happened with our team, but not, I don't think, in just two years. I've seen other coaches in this league— Mike Fratello comes to mind—be successful for five years being very intense. Then people said they got tired of listening to him. Well, he had to coach in his own way. Mike Schuler knew what he was doing and he was very successful.

I think things beyond Mike's control—the Vandeweghe situation, the change in ownership, the contract problems, the lack of talent in key spots—brought about his demise rather than his approach to the game or his personality.

You can't point the finger at just the players or the coach or management. But many times when tough situations arise, management's answer is to fire the coach. That's reality in professional sports.

October 12, 1990

Honolulu—We went into the first exhibition game against the Lakers with one thing in mind, to see what certain people could do. I was going to try to play Alaa as much as possible, and we wanted to play Cliff and Mark a lot. I wanted to give Danny Ainge the minutes he needed to get used to our system, and we wanted to see Shaun McDaniel to find out if he could help us.

Whether it was against the Lakers or anyone else, we had to accomplish certain things with our exhibition games.

But as the game started, it was pretty obvious that the players, even though they weren't in absolute top condition and weren't totally ready for the season to start, had an awful lot of pride riding on the game. You could see it from the very beginning.

Even though it was a meaningless exhibition game in Hawaii, it was still the Lakers vs. the Blazers. It was very competitive. The Lakers were intense. It was, after all, their first game under a new coach. But I went along with my substitution pattern in the first half just as I'd planned on doing. I wasn't going to extend anyone in the first exhibition game.

The game was close nearly all the way, and as the second half started, it was obvious the Lakers were going for the win. I was tempted to say, okay, we're going to throw everything out the window and go for it, too, if that's the way you want it. But I didn't do that. I felt I should stick to what our plan was.

We never did use McDaniel, but we played Clyde and Terry only thirty-three minutes apiece and used ten players. The Lakers used Magic Johnson for forty-two minutes, including the entire second half, and James Worthy played thirty-eight minutes. Down the stretch, they pulled away from us and beat us 119–115.

Afterward, there was a lot of disappointment. In fact, it was probably the most disappointment I have ever seen on a Trail Blazer team after a game we lost to the Lakers. And in an exhibition game, too.

I think it was because our players felt that if we had used our regular rotation and played our people as in a regular-season game, we would have won. But I also saw a lot of resolve. We play the Lakers again tomorrow night, and no way are we going to lose the next one. They aren't going to beat us two straight. It's taken us a couple of years, but at least we feel as if we're *supposed* to beat the Lakers.

When I got back to my room after the game, the red message light on my phone was blinking out of control. All kinds of writers wanted callbacks for preseason stories. It isn't just the coaching, as I said. It's the media, it's the fans, it's the demands of your own front office, and it's the pressure all of that brings that wears on you over the course of a season.

I sometimes wish it could just be basketball. When we started training camp, all I wanted to do was practice. But the first question is, "Are the practices going to be open to the media? To the public?" Okay, the practices are open to the media. So where do they sit? Where are you going to sit your own front office staff? You try to accommodate everyone, but some of it seems so ridiculous. All I want to do is practice.

Then in camp there's always the matter of making roster cuts. You can only carry twelve men on your team. Usually, because of the demands of the playoffs, the head coach doesn't really know too much about the players drafted in June. But they draft these players, give them to you, and now they're yours. You're responsible for them. I'm fortunate to have Bucky Buckwalter, our vice president/basketball operations, and Brad Greenberg, our director of player personnel, who are knowledgeable and experienced. They do a thorough job of constantly keeping the coaching staff updated on possible draftees.

Sometimes, whether the guy is good or not, if he doesn't quite succeed, it's because you didn't bring him along. It's because you didn't get this young talent to mature. And the guy simply may not be good enough. But everyone else is done with him now; he's yours.

Sometimes certain players don't play and people want to know why. It can be very irritating. Someone will say, "I think this guy should play more. He's a real talent." Never mind that you're winning or having a lot of success.

I'll get asked, why aren't you guys trapping more? Or, why aren't you running more set plays? Well, as the coach you know the personality of your team. You know what's good and what's not good. You welcome ideas or discussions, but it's still your job to coach the team. Obviously, if what you're doing doesn't work, you're going to be fired. If it does work, you're going to win and probably won't be fired.

I'm the head coach, and once I bring all these players into training camp, I'm responsible for them. Once you have your team, nobody else is responsible for anything. When a team fails, nobody goes back and says, well, maybe we didn't draft the right guy a few years ago, or maybe this player is slipping or that player isn't performing. It's always, let's change coaches and we can change the situation.

As a coach, I consider it essential to try to be positive all the time. I think, though, that the pressures of the job can make you more negative after a while.

What happened when I took this job was that the players saved me. They were supportive and never questioned anything I did. They responded. The only thing I asked of them was to play hard. There was a lot of turmoil, but I tried to do everything I could to get rid of that.

I learned a lot from Mike and Jack. I saw things that happened with both of them. But most important, you can't ever forget that this is a players' league. You've got to get your best players, your key players, to believe that you can help them succeed and that you can help them win. If you do that, they're going to bring the other guys with them.

I've felt comfortable from the very first day I took over the team. Some things I had to learn, but the important thing I learned at Chemeketa was that there's more to coaching than just drawing up plays. You need organizational skills and you need to get players to believe that what you do is the right way to do things. And you need to be able to deal with distractions, as I've said. The media's demands have really intensified this year, right from the start of training camp. Last season, it was mainly just the Portland media. Now, though, with a lot of people picking us to go all the way, I'm getting calls from all over the country. And not just newspapers, either; there are talk shows everywhere.

I'm lucky, because John Lashway and John Christensen of our public relations department help a lot, filtering the calls for me. They are the best in the NBA. That is very evident when you look at the job they did last year during the Finals. How they accommodated all the press in our building was amazing.

Our organization does a tremendous job with charities and fund-raising in our community. We're a good corporate citizen and our players are outstanding private citizens. But that brings with it continual demands. Players are required by their contracts to make a certain number of appearances, mandated by the club, per season. I don't think our organization has ever asked them to make as many as they could be required to make; the club tries hard not to do that.

But while the players aren't required to do many, the club is trying to get the players to do a lot of things on a voluntary basis. After games, we often have "walk-throughs" or get-togethers for our sponsors. The club wants to get the players to stop by for a few minutes on their way out of the arena. They want me to encourage the players to do this, but it's hard. I have to deal with the players in practice and the games; that should be enough. Keeping egos intact and trying to keep the people who aren't playing from being too unhappy, trying to keep everyone focused and in a positive frame of mind, is enough without having to talk a player into going somewhere he doesn't want to go. So I try not to get involved with too many things outside of basketball.

When things like that start entering into your relationship with a player, it affects that relationship. All it can do is destroy it. That's why I try not to get too involved in it. You don't need to make an issue over something that has nothing to do with your job, at least your main job of coaching the team. I mention certain things to them that I think are important to the community and the team, things that I believe they should do. And for the most part our players have been great, because of the type of people they are. They've gone along and are very giving of themselves within the community.

I learned at Chemeketa that I could get people to play for me, and I've always felt confident in that respect at the professional level. But you don't want to do too many things that can damage your rapport with players.

I was never frightened by the Blazer job. I was comfortable from the first day. I remember thinking, this must be what I'm supposed to be doing, because otherwise you get a sense of insecurity all the time. When I worked for Converse, selling shoes, I had that feeling. I wasn't comfortable with it. But I enjoyed the coaching job from the start. I also felt it would be just a matter of time before we would be successful. And if you have that confidence, it's going to come through to your players.

We had to try to think positive and play hard. The year I took over for Mike we didn't have a very good team at times. Our bench was two or three CBA players. But we played hard and tried to overcome our limitations; they busted their tails and we finally made the playoffs with an overtime win in the last game of the season.

I knew by then that I could coach. My biggest concern was whether I would be able to handle the distractions that go with coaching in the NBA. I really didn't know if I could do that. But once I got the job, I found I could.

I mean, I don't think I'm perceived as having the flashiest presence in the world, but I'm comfortable with who I am. I don't dress like Pat Riley or Chuck Daly and I never will. It's not that important to me. I want to look nice, but I'm not going to go out and buy eighty suits. I'd much rather have a sweat suit than a suit and tie.

I think I can present a pretty good image in the community. I have been part of it for the last fifteen years. I've raised my children here. And what is important, my wife and I chose to live here. I don't take myself all that seriously. I try to stay the same way I always was. Maybe people don't think I present a great image for TV or radio, but I do feel comfortable on the air and I even enjoy it.

I think I've surprised some people, including myself, with my ability to give speeches and talk to groups. I can do that.

But I don't think you have to put on airs or put on a show. People perceive me as being quiet and serious. This job is so much perception and hype that people can make you what- ever they want to make you. But I don't mind the way people perceive me. I don't have a problem with being laid-back or quiet. People figure that I just sit back and let my players play, let them do what they want to do.

Well, part of that is true. I think letting Terry Porter and Clyde Drexler go a little bit is a smart move. But there's no doubt in my mind that I'm in charge of the team. I think our track record is good. Obviously, letting those players do their thing works pretty well.

If I tried to harness those people, I don't think they'd be nearly as happy and they wouldn't be performing nearly as well.

If I had a different team, with players less athletic and gifted, I'd probably do it a different way. I did that in college. But this is a unique team with unique talents, and what's best for it is for me to step back and let them play. That's the bottom line and that's fine with me.

Coaches are important, but let's face it: the way they change coaches in the NBA, obviously there are plenty of them out there that teams can hire. It's the players who are the commodity in this league, and you have to understand that. It's not the coach. You can always get another coach. At least that's the feeling within the league.

I've made the tongue-in-cheek suggestion a few times that it would be easier to deal with all these guys if I were on their financial level. But that hasn't happened yet. And it never will. Coaches in the NBA make a good living, but we should—for what we have to put up with. It's a short-lived occupation, and sometimes, as I saw with Mike Schuler and Jack Ramsay, it's short-lived because of circumstances be- yond your control. Pat Riley made headlines with his $1- million-a-year contract, but that's still below average for NBA players. We're supposed to be the people in charge, but we make less money. I don't expect it to change—but can you blame me for wanting it to?

October 13, 1990

Honolulu—We used thirteen players against the Lakers in the rematch, with none of our starters playing more than twenty-nine minutes. Alaa Abdelnaby was our leading scorer with 16 points, and Shaun McDaniel played seven minutes, hitting all three of his field goals.

This game ended a lot different from the first. Magic played only twenty-two minutes, and the Lakers used just about everyone they had in uniform. We jumped them right at the start, and since they'd won the first game, they kind of changed and just substituted a lot of people.

We won the game 103–94 and I was relieved. These games don't mean anything, but still, they were two great challenges for us. I think these games solidified in our minds that we were going to be challenging the Lakers all year long.

They added Terry Teagle and Sam Perkins, two quality players, and these games made it clear they're going to be a tough rival. I think in the Pacific Division it's going to come down to us, the Lakers, and Phoenix. I think San Antonio is going to be right there with us in the overall Western Conference race.

October 14, 1990

Honolulu—It's a long flight home to Portland, but because of the win the night before, sleep comes a little easier. Sometimes I can't help but marvel at how far we've come in the last two seasons.

That first season we competed pretty well in the first round of the playoffs but still got blown out by the Lakers. The players were supportive, though, and whoever talked to our new owner, Paul Allen, and his assistant, Bert Kolde, about me from our front office had nice things to say about the job I did.

Paul could have come in and said, "Forget this," and gone out and gotten some well-known coach who was going to come in and change everything. But one of the things I've learned is that Paul really listens to his people, and if they make sense and are logical, he'll go along with them.

So I finally had the chance to coach my own NBA team, but it was an awful lot like the way things were when I played—a one-year contract, not a lot of security, and the constant feeling that my job was on the line every day.

There was no meeting, no discussion. I was offered a one-year contract, take it or leave it. I wasn't in any position to throw it out the window, but I felt I should at least have been given the opportunity to give my reasons why a multiyear contract would have been better.

The problem with a one-year contract for a coach of any professional team in any sport is that as soon as something negative happens, there's a good chance the players won't stick with you because they have more security than you have. It's no way to start a new situation, where you have to change things around.

You're grateful for the opportunity, but you understand what comes with it. And at the same time, I had always hoped I'd have a chance to negotiate my first contract.

During the off-season I went up to Bellevue, Washington, and met with Paul Allen and Bert Kolde. We talked about the team and what I was going to try to do with it. They asked if I had some concerns, and I brought up my problems with the one-year contract and asked them why they wanted it that way.

Basically, Paul said that when he bought the team, he was encouraged to give Mike Schuler a contract extension and he did. Then a short time later he ended up having to let him go. This time he wanted to be sure about his coach. He went along with the people who recommended he hire me, but he wanted to wait on anything more than one year.

I felt a lot better after hearing that. Certainly I didn't feel good about the one-year, but I felt good about finally getting the chance to sit down with him and tell him how I felt about it. I liked the dialogue. I think he listened to what I had to say, and I felt comfortable that he really was going to evaluate as we went along and be flexible enough to change if the situation merited it.

But I knew I didn't have a lot of time to make an impression. During that first training camp I wanted to do everything I could to create a different atmosphere. That's one reason we moved our camp out of town, to Salem. I still look back on that very first camp as the cornerstone of what we've built.

We needed to create a positive atmosphere and a new beginning. This was a team that had made the playoffs on the final day of the regular season the year before, then was run out of the playoffs in three straight games. But we had added Buck Williams and Wayne Cooper, and that made a huge difference. And we had a lot of young guys in that camp, too. We had a big meeting that first day and I just laid it on the line for everybody.

We weren't going to go along the same road we had traveled before, I told them. We were going to rededicate ourselves. This was a new camp with a new start; whatever happened in the past didn't exist anymore. The only way we were ever going to be successful was to put the past aside. If we didn't do that, we were going to have the same problems we always had. We were going to lose and everyone was going to be pointing fingers at each other.

We had been through enough of that already.

We also had to come to the realization, as a team, that unless we began to defend people, we were never going to win. I tried to point out that the successful teams won because when things got tough, they defended you. In the past, when things got tough for us, we fragmented. Everyone went his own way. We couldn't win that way.

I told them if there was a problem, it wasn't going to be discussed in the newspapers or among a hundred other people. If they had a problem, they were going to come to me with it. I told them I had a one-year contract and I wasn't going to sit there and lose and go through what had gone on the year before. If I was going to lose and be out of a job, I was going down doing it the way I wanted to do it.

Our players were ready for a change anyway. They had just about had it with everybody pointing fingers and jumping all over them. I think between bringing in Cliff Robinson and Byron Irvin as rookies, then adding Buck and Coop, we had added some real positive people with some energy, and that helped our core group of players—Clyde, Terry, Kevin Duckworth, and Jerome Kersey.

I wanted to change a couple of things out on the court. Defensively we had some really solid concepts that Mike had brought in from Milwaukee. I saw the value of them; we had rules for covering every possible defensive situation.

But the problem with those concepts was that there sometimes wasn't enough individual accountability. The idea was always to force your guy to the middle, or the baseline or whatever, where you had help.

I changed our tactics and challenged the players. Each man had to guard his guy a little better. We weren't going to worry so much about forcing people whichever way and expecting help; we were going to worry about each man doing a better job of guarding his own man.

That's about as simple as you can get. And there was accountability. Now we still sometimes decide we're going to play certain situations or plays a certain way. If you get beat, there should still be help coming. But we weren't going to give the players a crutch. We had gotten beat bad by penetration in the past. I wanted to take the alibis and excuses away. The primary purpose of the defense wasn't going to be to channel your man to where the help is supposed to be. The primary purpose is to *stop your man*.

Inside, too, we had been using crutches. Our big guys had begun to feel we were going to double-team everything inside so they didn't have to work as hard guarding their own man. I think Buck and Coop changed this philosophy as much as I did. The way they played, they wanted that accountability on themselves. They wanted to be responsible for taking someone on defensively. And they knew if someone got beat, they still had to help out.

We knew we weren't the greatest shooting team and that we needed some easy baskets. If we defended, and then if we rebounded, we were going to get some easy baskets. I believed those two areas were crucial. You can give them all the concepts in the world, but until they believed that defense and rebounding were the ways they were going to win, they weren't going to win.

And they did believe.

In that first training camp we did some things differently with the team. But I did some things differently, too, on the executive level.

The first thing I did after I got the job was to fly up to Seattle to talk to Paul and Bert. I wanted them to have a chance to know me personally. I don't see how anybody can deal with another person without the chance to know him. If I was going to go down there and coach Paul's team, I wanted him to know what kind of person I was.

And I wanted there to be no mistake about what I was trying to do and what my philosophy was. He was going to know why I did certain things and why I didn't do others. I felt it was better for me to do that than to have some middleman do it; I didn't want him to rely on what he read in the paper about the team or what someone else told him. If I was going to get fired in that first year, it was going to be because of what I did, not because of someone else's interpretation of what I did or didn't do.

Larry Weinberg, our previous owner, was a perceptive man and was also a great fan. He and his family were very interested in the team and the league. Paul Allen is much the same. He is a great basketball fan and is very interested in finding out all he can about the game and why we do things a certain way. I have enjoyed and appreciated the chances I have had to talk to him about basketball and the coaching staff's goals and aspirations for the team. At least he gets to know me and can see what we are trying to do and what we are facing.

Another important thing we did with the players goes all the way back to my playing career. When I was a player, I knew I couldn't do a lot of things. I wasn't a great player, I was a role player. But some things I did pretty well, too. I was never going to be a great shooter, and I was never able to go down the floor and defend someone fullcourt. But I could defend in the halfcourt. And I could pass the ball and get my team into its offense. I could get the ball to the shooters.

Coaches always look at the negatives. They always look at what a player can't do, rather than what he can do. I resolved never to do that.

Kevin Duckworth is a classic example. He's not the greatest rebounder in the world, and he's never going to be a shot-blocker. People get so down on him because of this. But you have to look at what he *can* do.

We tried to tell him not to get down on himself. And we tried not to make him into something he isn't. What he can do defensively is fill: he can fill a lot of space and he's quick. He gets to spots and stops penetration and he does it well. But there are no statistics to prove this, so he doesn't get any credit for doing something important and difficult on defense. But I know he does it, and I make sure he knows that.

He also doesn't get a lot of rebounds, but if he can keep his guy from getting great position on him, use his size to keep people out, he's doing his job. We have Buck, Jerome, and Clyde to do the bulk of rebounding. That's what they do well.

Another great example of this is Clyde. I'll admit there are times when I hear people say, jeez, Clyde's not the greatest shooter in the world, and sometimes his shot selection isn't the best. And he'll go for steals sometimes at the defensive end when he shouldn't. Those things can be said about a lot of players, but with Clyde people might dwell on those things because of his impact on the team.

Because of his abilities, he is always your best chance to turn the team around. If things don't go well, it's so easy for people to say, if he would only do this a little better, we could be a whole lot better. But that's a dangerous trap for a coach, to forget that even your best player is a human being and not a machine.

You have to look at the whole picture. Some things I'd

love to have him do better, but no perfect players are around. And if you step back and take a look at Clyde, you'll see that nobody but Michael Jordan can do the things Clyde can do. He can rebound, he can get easy baskets for you. Very few guys can get easy baskets for your team the way Clyde can.

So I try to look at those strengths and to build on them. He isn't as good an outside player as some other guys, but he makes big outside shots at crucial times—because he has the courage to take those big shots. He makes enormously key shots at crucial times and breaks a team's back with them. He has great belief in himself.

I think with a player such as Clyde you have to let him go and put him in an arena that's best for him. Let him use his skills in ways that help the team.

People forget where he came from. He came out of Houston a year early and had a tough time as a rookie. He was playing behind Jim Paxson, who was a second-team all-pro. I think in some ways that probably helped Clyde, even though it was difficult for him at the time. I think if he had gotten to play a lot as a rookie for a bad team, he may have had the kind of problems I saw Sidney Wicks develop when he first came to Portland.

Wicks was drafted by the Trail Blazers my second year there, and he was a great, great player. But as an explosive rookie on a team without a lot of scoring options, he was expected to carry a big load. He did, averaging 25 points, 10 rebounds, and 4 or 5 assists, but the team was losing and he drew a lot of the blame. That's what happens to a high-profile player on a bad team; people start saying you aren't a leader, you can't do this or that. It killed Sidney. He started focusing on his statistics as the only way for him to prove his worth in the league. It's really sometimes better for a rookie to come into the league on a good team where there's less pressure on him, where he can take some time and develop. I think that's what happened with Clyde that first year. But that doesn't mean it was easy.

I remember one confrontation during his rookie season,

which was also my rookie year as an assistant coach. He was going through a tough adjustment and he wasn't playing. Everyone who knows him knows how competitive he is and how that must have affected him.

We were practicing during the all-star break in San Diego. A lot of us stayed there during the break because we were going to play Los Angeles. We were scrimmaging, and as all assistants have to do, I was in charge of officiating the game—which is a no-win situation. You can't make the right call for every player.

And Clyde was frustrated. He took a shot and thought he was fouled, but I didn't make a call. He got real upset. Then after another play he got even more upset and turned and said something to me. I said something back like, just play the game, Clyde. And he really went off on me.

I said something to him like, have some respect, and he countered with, "You've got to earn respect." I said, that's right, you do. Jack just let it go; he never said a word. It was between me and Clyde. And both of us were really frustrated.

It really bothered me because as an assistant coach you do want their respect, and it was my first year coaching in the NBA. After practice I went back to the hotel and talked to Mary Kay about it. We talked and I thought about it, and I began to see that it really stemmed from Clyde's frustration at not playing. He wasn't really upset at me as much as at his own situation. As it happened, I was walking through the hotel lobby later that day and he was on his way out. I went up to him and said, we're in this together, Clyde. I was sorry and so was he.

I think that set a tone between us. I could have been ticked off and just said, hey, that son of a gun has no right to say that to me. I'm one of the coaches. I remember it still so vividly because he was so upset. But we talked it out and everything was fine after that. Sometimes that happens and you've got to understand it's going to happen. His game has improved a lot since he came into the league. But I think you have to let him play. You can't put restraints on him because you don't know when he's going to come up with those amazing plays. He's the type of guy who within a five-minute period can change a game. And if you start putting restrictions on him, he's not going to have those spurts.

His instincts are tremendous. I don't think there's a better open-court passer in the league than Clyde. He's so unselfish. And I don't think there's a better rebounding guard in the league, either.

But some people said he was difficult to coach.

I have been asked this question a thousand times about how coachable Clyde is. Well, he has been great with me. When you are coaching, I believe you go only on what has happened between you and the player—not on what has happened in the past or on what you have heard. Clyde has done everything I have asked of him. He has sacrificed more than any other player for the good of the team. His scoring average has dropped 5 points a game in two years because our team has more firepower—not because he can't still score 27 points per game. He has helped our younger players in a quiet way. The situations before I was coach were overblown.

Jack Ramsay's situation with Clyde was different from Mike Schuler's. Jack had no problems with Clyde. Clyde was young and wanted to prove he could play in the NBA. But Jack had Paxson, and then, the next year, he had Kiki Vandeweghe at small forward. Paxson was an all-pro for Jack and he wasn't going to hand that spot over immediately to Clyde. And we had traded half a team for Kiki, so he had to play. But then Clyde burst on the scene.

I don't really think when we drafted Clyde very many people thought he was going to be the type of player he has turned out to be. They thought he was a tremendous talent, but at that time, we didn't even know if he was going to be a guard or a forward. And he was so young, it was hard to tell how he would mature.

It was obvious, though, he was a much more gifted athlete than Kiki or Pax. They were both hardworking players who shot the ball well. They were sound fundamentally and just different kinds of players from Clyde, who was so much better an athlete than either one of them. Jack saw his talent and Clyde began to play more and more.

It was just a question of circumstances with Jack. But with Mike, well, it's really hard to describe it. Mike felt that if Clyde would play a little differently, we would be even more successful. He wanted Clyde to take a little different approach to the game, too. It was really two guys with separate visions of what kind of player Clyde should be. Mike had one idea and Clyde had another. Mike felt Clyde could be more of a leader on and off the floor. He had coached Sidney Moncrief at Milwaukee and Sidney was a great leader there. Mike was hoping Clyde could be the same type of leader in Portland. Clyde and Sidney, however, are two different people. Clyde leads with his play. He goes about things quietly. He is more likely to talk with players in a one-on-one situation than in a group. There are many types of leaders and ways to do it.

The situation was different after we acquired Buck Williams. Terry Porter came into his own, too. I think the overall maturation of our team changed things. We don't need Clyde to be anyone but himself.

October 20, 1990

Klamath Falls, Oregon—Every season we play at least one exhibition game in a small town in Oregon. We've played in Coos Bay, Pendleton, Medford, Corvallis, Eugene, and here, near the California border at the Oregon Institute of Technology gym.

I think it's great for the people in those places who never otherwise get a chance to see us play. Whatever gym it is, we usually sell it out, and it's a really enthusiastic place. The only problem with the games is that in some seasons we played in several of the towns, complicating our preseason with a lot of time on a bus. That means you lose quality practice time.

A couple of these games is fine, but any more than that and you're hopping around the state and not getting anything done. The time in October is the only time all year you get any concentrated practice time, and you have a lot to get done. You don't want to spend a lot of that time sitting on a bus or a little commuter plane. Plus those gyms are always a little smaller than the regular NBA playing floor, and that isn't good, either.

But I love playing in those little gyms because of the fans. We pounded Sacramento in this game and the fans were terrific—so enthusiastic and so excited to see us play. The people sit right on top of the action, and it's almost like a high school atmosphere.

Mark Bryant got into a fight during this game with a player of theirs who we all knew had no chance of making the Kings' roster. Mark punched the guy and I'm afraid the league might take action against him. It's a tough call. A lot of things were going on as the players ran up and down the court and it just happened.

October 31, 1990

Portland—We're going to open up the season the day after tomorrow, without Mark Bryant. The league suspended him for one game because of his fight in the exhibition season. The guy he got into the fight with was cut, and I'm wondering what the league would have done had he been at fault—suspend him from a game in Europe? Because Mark has a guaranteed contract, they can suspend him.

I'm pleased with how the training camp has gone. We competed hard and I sense we're ready for the regular season. More important, Buck followed Clyde's lead and reached a contract agreement. Only Jerome is left, and I think that will happen soon.

A lot of other people sense we're ready for the season, too, because every time I pick up a preseason publication, someone is picking us to win it all. That, of course, isn't news to our fans. They've been picking us since the Finals ended last June.

It didn't take long for Danny Young to prove that Shaun McDaniel wasn't consistent enough and didn't shoot the ball well enough to beat him out for a roster spot. Shaun had done well in the summer league, but he made too many mistakes. Danny just played better than he did.

I was pleased with Alaa Abdelnaby. I didn't know how he was going to be; in the summer league he was inconsistent, and when I looked back at most of our other players—Clyde, Jerome, Terry, Fat Lever—they had been head and shoulders above everyone else in summer league. Alaa was not really a factor. Seven points a game. Two rebounds and, because they had a no-foulout rule, eight fouls a game. But I think he took a backseat to Cliff and Mark, who were also there, so he didn't get a chance to do what he could do. I think he stood back and didn't want to rain on their parade. But in training camp he turned it all around. He looks as if he can play.

He was an unusual case, however. Usually it's like McDaniel, where you see a guy in the summer and think he's better than he is, because of the caliber of competition. With Alaa, it was different. He was better in training camp against our good players. It's an encouraging sign.

November

November 2, 1990

Portland—A lot of people don't remember it now. It's kind of just drifted away and I've never brought it up in any newspaper stories, but toward the end of my career as a player for the Trail Blazers, in the team's second season, I couldn't do much of anything right.

I was booed all the time. It's one thing I remember and one thing I know Mary Kay remembers—because she used to have to sit in the stands and listen to it.

My first year as a Blazer was great. We had Leroy Ellis, Jim Barnett, Geoff—and nothing was expected of us and there was no pressure. We ran a passing-game offense under Rolland Todd and got a lot of easy shots. I couldn't come off screens and hit jump shots—it just wasn't my game. The free-flowing passing game was terrific for me. But later, under Jack McCloskey, we were a lot more structured and I basically just got the ball to Geoff or Sidney Wicks and got the hell out of the way.

I still remember standing there, making a pass to one of those guys and having some fan behind me scream, "Adelman, will you move? Do something." And I felt like turning around and saying, this is my job. This *is* what I am supposed to do.

I wasn't the greatest shooter and I didn't score much. So I was kind of the guy the fans picked out. I became the reason we were losing. It bothered me a lot, and it bothered my play. It eventually was the reason that I didn't come to training camp a year later. I knew Chicago was interested in me, and I didn't want to come back to Portland to go through that again. I don't think Jack thought I was going to be an effective player for him, anyway.

When I look back on it, I realize it was just a few individuals in the stands. But that's all it takes when there's only five thousand people at the game and you're not winning. But see, people were not looking at what I could do—they were looking at what I couldn't do.

Actually, our experience in Portland was a positive one. Around town people treated us great. I just hated coming to the game. Those same people were always sitting in the same seats.

I still remember this one guy. I don't remember his name, but I've talked to him since. Back then he used to sit in the front row. He was on me all the time. No matter what, whenever I made a mistake, he would jump up and scream and yell at me, right there from the front row.

Finally, one time I picked the ball up—it was our ball out of bounds—and he started screaming at me again. I just turned around and handed him the ball and said, you go do it. If you can do it better, go ahead. He sat down and never said another word to me the rest of the season.

I guess I don't understand people who have to do that. I can see people getting upset; they pay their money and I understand that. I can see people booing the team if the players aren't performing or working hard. But to get on one individual no matter what, I'll never understand that. I was trying as hard as I could. I was doing everything I thought I could do.

It seemed almost as if it were all premeditated. They

had already made up their minds they were coming to the game to boo—and then they just waited for their first opportunity.

I was losing confidence in almost every game. And that's the unfortunate part of professional sports. When you make mistakes, everyone in the world knows about it. Somebody might make a mistake in their office and their boss might know about it, or somebody next to them might know about it. But in sports, everybody in the world knows and they're all going to remind you of it.

That's what makes it really hard. But when I came back to coach at Chemeketa, the thing that amazed me is how many people remembered my playing in Portland. I mean, I'm not six foot eight and I didn't have any kind of brilliant career there or anything. But it didn't matter where we went in the state, someone would say, "Hey, aren't you . . ." or "Didn't you used to . . ." And the old bitterness melted away.

I think that's how the people in Oregon are. Any player who comes back seems to get a big hand from the fans. There's a real sense of community here. That's the flip side of the pressure we sometimes feel from the fans' intense focus on the team. I should try to remember that more.

We opened the 1990–91 season with a rough night.

They unfurled the Western Conference championship banner in Memorial Coliseum before the game against Houston, and it always seems that teams don't play well on those nights. Someone told me the Lakers lost three straight games on the nights they had their ring ceremonies. They lost the games because their minds were on other things.

I think this game will be good for us because it kind of woke us up. Houston could have beaten us. Danny Ainge came in and gave us a big lift. We were down 75–65 and finally won 90–89. We made a big surge, got 11 points ahead, and then didn't score for the final three minutes of the game. They had the ball for the final shot, and we switched all their screens and they didn't get it to Kenny Smith. David Wood missed the shot at the end.

It was a little scary because there is so much hype going into this game about us winning the championship. I think this game reminded us that it isn't going to be easy. We found out we have to play much better than this or we aren't going to be challenging in the West.

November 3, 1990

Sacramento—If we learned any lessons against Houston the previous night, they didn't show tonight. Clyde went 1 for 16 from the floor. We shot awful from the field and nothing went right. We shouldn't even have been in the game. We trailed them most of the second half, and I think we suffered a little from having thumped them twice during the exhibition season; I guess we figured there was no way they could stay with us.

Clyde was having a tough offensive game, but then, and I don't know where he came from, out of nowhere he came flying and blocked a shot by Lionel Simmons that would have won the game for them at the end. We ended up winning 95–93 in overtime.

Simmons caught the ball in the corner, and it looked as if he had a dead-open shot to win the game, and Clyde just smothered it. Clyde has that ability. He can be 1 for 16 or whatever and still come up with the big play that will break the other team's back. And it doesn't matter what kind of play it is.

Those first two games were about as bad as you can get. We played so poorly, and yet we're 2–0. It's got to get better. It just can't go on like this.

November 6, 1990

Los Angeles—This is the first game of the season against the Lakers that counts, and both Jerome Kersey and Cliff Robinson got hurt in it. Jerome had an unusual day; he finally reached an agreement on a lucrative contract extension during the day, and then he went right out and took a horrible fall that will probably be shown on replay for years to come. It looked as if he broke his neck, but we think he'll be okay in a couple of days. Cliff suffered a sprained ankle.

We were 6 points behind with a minute and a half to go in regulation when Clyde hit a 3-pointer. After a Laker miss, we were trying to set up a little pick-and-roll situation looking for a quick 3. If we didn't have a wide-open look at a 3, we wanted to take the ball to the basket hard and see if we couldn't get 2 for sure, and maybe draw a foul. Terry turned the corner and went really hard to the hole. A.C. Green just reacted, tried to come over and was a step late, and Terry finished the play, got fouled, and tied the game and put it into overtime.

We got down again, but Terry hit an 18-foot jumper with 11.6 seconds left in overtime to win it 125–123. And I think this game just might set us off.

We had played so poorly in our first two games. The Lakers had lost their opening game in San Antonio. This was the kind of game we could never win in the past at Los Angeles. Never. We would probably lose because we had won two and they were coming in for their home opener. But we just wouldn't go away, and I think it was a big lift for us.

We got lucky in the first two games and people were saying, what's wrong? I think our home opener was just circumstances, and the second game we felt we were going to beat Sacramento pretty easily because we had really whipped them during the exhibition season. But this game we got up for and we came back and won it. It was a great win. And the funny thing is, everybody's already asking, what's wrong with the Lakers? I think it's a little early for that.

November 9, 1990

Portland—It's so early in the season and the world champion Detroit Pistons are already back in town. The big rematch is what the fans were calling it.

We were determined to set the defensive tone against them. We felt we could defend them better than we did in the Finals, but we had to be the aggressors. The loss to the Pistons in the Finals, especially those three games in Portland, are still very fresh in our minds. We want to prove we're an improved team from last season and to erase the memory of that loss in the Finals.

It's funny, but going into the game I never doubted we were going to win. I thought they would come in and think that they were just going to win, that they had our number. But we were ready from the start and I just never worried about it. We were good. We blew them away and won 113–101 in a game that wasn't nearly as close as the final score says it was.

Looking back to the Finals, I think there is such a fine line between winning and losing those four games we lost—except for the first game at home, when they really beat us pretty good. But we could easily have won the other three or won at least one of them. I thought what we were doing against them was good, and I still think we match up well with them.

November 10, 1990

Portland—We had a light practice today at the Jewish Community Center. Our routine is nearly always the same. I always try to remember that you have twelve individuals on your team and they all have a part. You have to keep in mind that you have to go to some of them at key times and keep them going, because they're not all getting what they want. Some people are really sacrificing themselves to play a certain role.

Sometimes you forget that, but I try to get to guys before practice and talk with them. If you don't make a point of talking with them one-to-one, weeks can go by and pretty soon you have a problem. Sometimes guys just need to talk to you about things. Before practice is a great time for it. Our guys are just shooting and I try to move around and chat.

Then, before we start, we always get together in the middle of the floor. I try to talk to them about the standings, or what the upcoming week or group of games means to them. Or sometimes I'll just talk about what we'll do that day in practice. I think you always need to get them together before you start, just to get them all focused.

If you've played the night before, you want to keep it light early in the practice. You don't want this to be drudgery. It doesn't always have to be a painful thing to practice. Then at the end of the workout, I bring everyone together again. You always just want to start and end on the right foot.

We probably practice less than most teams in the NBA. And when we do practice, we don't practice as long. I think you have to be careful in this league, especially as the season goes along, that you aren't wearing out your players. If we aren't playing well, at times I know we need to practice, but I try to balance that with the need for the players to get their legs back and heal minor injuries. We have very well-conditioned players. I don't want to break them down.

We never practice after back-to-back games. I think it's important that my players know that. Even if we lose a couple of games, I want them to know that they can look at the schedule and have some days without practicing at all. Psychologically, that's probably more important than anything we could accomplish out on the floor. We might have a team meeting or something if we're in a rough period, but I don't believe in punishing players with practice.

If I had a younger team, I would probably feel a little differently. They would probably need more practices. But a veteran team needs its legs more than a practice. Besides, I know my team usually responds well after a day off.

After beating Detroit our confidence level was really high. People don't understand about the eighty-two-game schedule in our league; you're going to have some games where you're going to play poorly, and we happened to have them in our first two. The Lakers are having them in their first seven. But if you're a good team, it's not going to last. You're eventually going to get the schedule going your way and get some confidence. Back-to-back wins against the Lakers and Detroit leave you feeling pretty good. And I'm sure the guys will be up for tomorrow's game—Mike Schuler's coming into town.

November 11, 1990

Portland—Mike had taken over the Clippers and he brought them into Memorial Coliseum for the first time. We just dominated them from the start. It was 136–107 and it was as if they never had a chance. Any time old teammates or coaches play each other the game seems to have special meaning, particularly the first time they meet.

The Clippers have a lot of young talent, but they've been snakebitten time after time by injuries. They need to get Ron Harper back. If he can come back from his serious knee injury, they can be a very good team. If Mike is given the time, he will win in Los Angeles.

Teams need to keep a group together and let them mature and grow as a unit. We kept a core group and built around it. I believe the Clippers are close to putting it all together. But you need patience and to make the right trade that solidifies your team. If you get lucky, it all comes together.

It's better to have a mixture of veterans and promising young players than to have either all veterans or all young players like the Clippers. Another problem they've had is that too many of their good young players have played the same position—forward. I think a healthy Ron Harper could be a key for the Clippers. But you need leadership from your veterans.

November 13, 1990

Portland—We were 5–0 and had Denver up next, and I was worried about this game. I watched them on tape against Phoenix, and everyone was scoring big on them. People were talking about a 200-point game. I was worried they were going to score a lot of points and we were going to get really lax and just try to match them basket for basket. And I was worried about turning the ball over.

It's hard to understand about coaches. We worry, especially when we haven't played against a team that has a new coach, a new system, and a lot of new players. I mean, Phoenix had just scored 180 points against them. I just didn't have any idea what to expect. When you're coaching, you worry about everything, but especially about the unknown.

But once it started . . . We just threw the ball over the top of their presses. Once I saw the game and the way it started and the way our guys were, I knew it was just a matter of how many points we were going to score. For the record, we won 155–129. You let us throw it over the top to Clyde or Jerome Kersey to finish at the other end and you have no chance.

I think this game—not the Lakers and Pistons games, which I knew we'd be up for—showed me just how good we can be. I had watched tape of Phoenix dismantling Denver, and we did the same thing; we just took them apart. I worried we might get a little casual and not be intelligent, but maybe I underestimated my team a little bit.

I think the Nuggets are going to have to change the way they play. Too many teams in the league can finish plays on them—it's just too easy. Then you know their guys will eventually get discouraged.

The system worked fine for Paul Westhead at Loyola Marymount. But I think one big problem they have with it in the NBA is that they can't draw the charging fouls like they do in the college game. In college you can step in front, take the charge, and even if they pass the ball off to someone else, you can still get the call. In our league, the refs won't make that call. And you can jump in there under the basket for a charge and people will just dunk it over you.

After about six games, you're not going to step in anymore. It's a different game in the pros.

What they really need is a shotblocker. And what Paul really needs for his system is quality players. That's what any system needs. It will be interesting to see what Denver does this season.

Many people don't remember, but our very first coach in Portland, Rolland Todd, was probably the first guy to initiate the passing game in the NBA. I don't remember any team running it the way we did that first year in Portland with our expansion team. And he had great success using a small lineup—the same thing Don Nelson did so successfully many years later. Doug Moe did a lot of the same things at Denver.

It was Todd's whole offense in Portland, and no one had really done that before. I really enjoyed it, and it was probably the most fun I ever had as a player. We just tried to outscore the other team and didn't pay a whole lot of attention to defense. We played some exciting basketball.

We ran a lot of really good teams right out of our building. We were a first-year expansion team, but we beat Boston, New York, Baltimore, Atlanta. And we were using Jim Barnett, at six foot four, at small forward, and Shaler Halimon, six five, at power forward, along with Geoff and me at guard and Leroy Ellis, who was six eleven but a perimeter player, at center. We ran teams right off the floor.

We had all kinds of trouble guarding teams, but they couldn't guard us, either. We pushed the ball upcourt, moved it around, and played a very up-tempo game all the way. We ended up winning 29 games. It got me a chance to score in double figures; it must have been a pretty good system if I could score 12 points a game.

But after that first year the team made the decision to go with younger players and we traded away Ellis and Barnett.

They were two of our top scorers. Then Geoff got hurt and we were minus our three leading scorers, and it left Sidney Wicks as the only guy who could score. We just didn't have the same type of personnel, and we couldn't run the way we did before.

Our whole game changed and we couldn't run the passing game anymore. It was too bad. I think sometimes you need to stay with things just a little longer. Perhaps Denver will. But I still think their presses make things too easy.

November 15, 1990

Portland—The Knicks came into town next, riding a four-game win streak, including a win over the Lakers in Los Angeles. But we were so confident and so ready for the game. We were just on a roll at this time, and we wanted to show our stuff to one of those power teams from the East. Whenever you play the Knicks you know that all the media attention will be there. The Knicks have a way of bringing out the best in us, I think.

We scored on 11 of our first 12 shots from the floor, 8 of them from the outside. I can't remember a game where we shot the ball well from the outside and got beat. When we do that, or if we get too many easy baskets, we're going to win.

We won this one 141–125 and had the Knicks shaking their heads. They were just overmatched in this game.

Before the game Drazen Petrovic spoke out in the newspapers and said he wanted to be traded or he would go back to Yugoslavia. We fined him $500, which was later rescinded when he apologized.

A lot of people, including those in the media, didn't agree with us for fining him. This is America, it was said, and he should be able to say what he wants to say. But I think a precedent had to be set because I had talked to him I don't know how many times about his situation. Geoff Petrie had talked to him about it. We were both very clear on where he stood.

He's upset that he's not playing more. I mean, I'm sorry, but Terry, Clyde, and Danny Ainge are better players. It's that simple. I don't think he can play point guard as well as our two Dannys. He's our fifth guard; that's just the way it is.

I think most of the players didn't think he should be fined, either. But it wasn't the fact that he wanted either to play or be traded; I could understand that. It was threatening to leave the team and go home to Yugoslavia. Look, either you're part of this team or you're not. I think the team had to say something. If he and his agent wanted to go public, then we had to do something and not just let it die.

By this time, I had just about had it with the Drazen Petrovic situation anyway. When you're 6–0 and playing as well as we're playing, you shouldn't have to worry about this kind of thing. If we were 3–3 or 2–4 and he was upset, he might have a case. But not then. Or if we were 20 games into the season and he said something, then maybe I would have bought it a little bit. But six games into the season?

I feel sorry for Drazen that he wasn't allowed to come into this league and learn about it and feel his way through it. Everyone expected him to just come over here and be Pete Maravich. That was the term used. I hate people comparing new players to older or even current players in the league because it's ridiculous. I mean, I played with Pete Maravich. I knew the minute I saw Petrovic he was not going to be Pete Maravich. It was unfair to Drazen. It put a lot of pressure on him and he felt it. He had been a star in Europe, and people felt he had to come over and be a star here, too.

The one thing I will say for Petro is that through all the stuff he was a great guy for our team. He worked harder than anyone in practice. As much as he could, he kept his head up. He was very positive.

But I knew after the exhibition season that Danny Ainge was better for our team and he was going to play. And I didn't think that defensively I could play Danny and Drazen together a lot. I thought we could do it on occasion, but I wanted to keep a defensive tone to our team, and a lot of people don't realize that Danny plays pretty good defense. But if you play Danny and Drazen together, you get away from what Danny does best because he's going to have to handle the ball most of the time, and that takes away some of his energy for the defensive end.

And the biggest problem with Drazen was that he was used to having the ball in his hands all the time. He was used to being a scorer off the dribble. The game always revolved around him and he just wasn't going to have that on our team. He had to change his game and it isn't easy for players to do that. I also knew he was a good offensive player and we didn't want to just get rid of him. I knew he wasn't going to play a lot and that I was going to have to deal with that.

The one thing I resented more than anything was that his agent, Warren LeGarie, told Drazen to make the statement, thinking he could force us to trade him or play him. He was saying things about our team and about me, saying I was lying. He said I didn't like Drazen and it was totally untrue. And this was a guy, this agent, whom I hadn't talked to in two years about Drazen.

He never once talked to me about his client—which was okay, because I probably wouldn't have talked to him anyway. I don't make a habit of talking to agents about playing time for their players. I will talk to them if the players are upset and they just want to know where he's at. But LeGarie never had the courage to even ask me about it. He went through other people, and to the papers and the talk shows. He said a lot of things that were totally unfounded, and all he did in the long run was hurt Drazen. That's all he did. Drazen had always been everybody's favorite, and he put him in a bad situation. And I think he did him a disservice.

It was tough on Drazen because part of being in this business is learning to deal with the adversities as well as the good times. I don't believe Drazen had ever had to handle much adversity until he came here. And he was never allowed to fight through it.

I don't have a problem with a guy who says he wants to

play. If he didn't want to play, he wouldn't belong in this league. But Drazen knew the situation and we couldn't do much about it. His agent's making statements wasn't going to change anything.

Everybody wants to play. Other guys sitting on the bench want to play just as badly as you do. But if you continue to talk about leaving, you won't be a part of the group anymore. No one person is bigger than the team.

November 17, 1990

Denver—Our rematch with the Nuggets went the same way as the previous game. I think they thought maybe we would play differently in their building or maybe they could do a little bit more, but they shot horribly. We jumped all over them again. They shot great in the third quarter but couldn't make up any ground because they weren't stopping us at all. Jerome and Clyde love playing them. It was lay-up after lay-up. Jerome had 8 assists in this game—and that's unusual because he's usually a scorer, not a passer, in our fastbreak. But the assist total reflected our ball movement and activity as a team. They pressed us and we ended up with a lot of 2-on-1s, with Jerome dishing off to the open man. I wasn't as worried about them this time because I knew what they would try to do, and I figured we could defend them well. And I didn't think they could defend us. This was eight in a row for us.

We have to go home and play the Chicago Bulls tomorrow night, but back-to-back games are a much easier task than they used to be, thanks to our leased airplane, *Blazer I*. It's a BAC-111, a plane that seats twenty-two but was originally built to accommodate about three times that many. We have captain's chairs, plenty of legroom, and great service. We decide when we want to leave, and we don't have to hassle at the main airport. We fly out of small airports that are much easier to get in and out of.

After the game at Denver we were home in our beds before

one o'clock in the morning. We use a small airport at Hillsboro, just west of Portland, near where a lot of the players live. You park your car, walk twenty feet, and get on the plane.

We have VCRs so the players can look at movies and we can look at game tapes. The coaches have one quiet area in the front where we can talk about what we're going to do. The players have another cabin in the back. They get great food and terrific service. It's been a big bonus, too, that they're all together after games—talking about the games. It's really been great for camaraderie.

We can go to such cities as Seattle, Sacramento, Oakland, and Salt Lake City on the day of the game. We don't always have to go a day ahead. I think the less amount of time you have to spend on the road, the better off you are. After games on the West Coast, we can usually come home right after the game. It's much better than having to get up early the next morning to take a commercial flight.

I think chartering or owning your own plane can really help a good team that already believes it has an excellent chance to win on the road. We feel *Blazer I* gives us a big advantage. But if you don't have a good team, I don't think a supersonic jet is going to help you win any games.

November 18, 1990

Portland—This is our second game in two nights, but at least it's at home. One of the things that really surprises me is that neither of our games against Chicago is scheduled for national television. It's obvious that no one realizes how competitive our games are with them and that the matchup between Clyde and Michael Jordan is a classic. Here we are playing Chicago, and both teams are playing for the second night in a row. This game ought to be a showcase game. If anybody had watched our two teams play each other in the last two years, they would have seen some great basketball. It surprises me that no one realizes this. It makes me angry.

You have two teams that could make a hell of a game for somebody to watch on national television and it's being played on Sunday night.

For the limited number of people who got to see it, we put on another terrific show. Again, we shot the ball well. That's the thing about our start—I don't know if we can shoot the ball any better than we have been. We shot over 60 percent against Denver, we shot great against New York, and we shot 62 percent against the Bulls. Duck had a great game, going 10 for 13. They have a tough time guarding him. It was our fourth straight game over 60 percent. And against the Bulls, that's saying something.

But by now we were in such a flow, playing with complete confidence. We won the game 125–112, although they made a run at us in the second half. Still, shooting more than 60 percent against a team that plays solid defense—it was an accomplishment.

Danny Ainge is off to a terrific start. Nine games into the season and he's shooting 61 percent from the floor. And they're all jump shots. I don't think in his wildest dreams he thought it was going to be this easy at the start. He made everything he shot.

We felt last summer that we needed an experienced guard off the bench who could score. A lot of names were out there; Danny and Ricky Pierce were the guys we really wanted. We couldn't ever get anything done with Pierce. The Bucks kept talking as if they wanted to trade him, but either they didn't really want to or we didn't have what they wanted. But Sacramento wanted our draft pick and had some interest in Byron Irvin. We needed someone who could step in and play and we didn't need another young player. I think it worked out.

People around town are beginning to talk about the possibility of our winning 70 games. That's crazy, but . . . when you look at this start, beating the Lakers in L.A., then Detroit, New York, and Chicago at home, we're really on a roll. We aren't just beating good teams by a couple of points. We're dominating people.

As we head into Thanksgiving, I have two special things to be thankful for: my family and the opportunity to coach this basketball team.

Just to have the opportunity to coach in the NBA is a great honor; to have the good fortune of coaching an outstanding team is special. Our players have worked very hard to get to this point. Some of them have struggled through some tough seasons. Seeing them come together in such a close-knit manner, to where they truly enjoy playing and have become such good friends, is unique in this business. It's what you dream about as a coach.

In a little more than a year we've taken a very fragmented team and turned it into one of the best in the league. We've responded to the pressure of being picked to win the championship by jumping off to the best start in the NBA. That was our first goal: to get off to a quick start and take advantage of our home schedule in November. And we've done it.

It has gone through my mind that we've shot the ball so well in this stretch that we may be fooling ourselves a little. What will happen when we hit a stretch where we don't shoot well? The one thing I take comfort in is that our success isn't just based on our shooting. It's also our defense and rebounding.

Still, when we shoot like this we're not going to lose very many games.

November 23, 1990

Portland—Golden State came into town and we just destroyed them, too. It wasn't even close. We were up 24 at halftime after outscoring them 41–16 in the second quarter. After the Chicago game, you'd think we'd be a little bit down, but we beat the Warriors 143–119 to go 10-0. I don't think anybody expected that to happen. You may win games, but not the way we are winning them.

November 25, 1990

Portland—Everything that led up to this game was nothing compared to the San Antonio game. Damn, I was totally amazed in the first quarter, as was everyone else.

We scored 11 of the first 12 points of the game, and it was coming more from our defense than our offense. We were so alive on defense it was frightening. We led 28–9 halfway through the quarter, then went crazy in the final two minutes of the period to lead 49–18 after the period.

There were so many spectacular plays, most of them involving Clyde or Jerome—who were flying. Drexler blocked 4 shots in the first quarter, made 7 of his 8 shots, had 4 assists and 2 steals, en route to 15 points. We made 22 of 25 shots and hit all 5 of our 3-point field goals.

We were stuffing them at one end, flying out on the fast break, and either finishing plays with dunks or pulling up and nailing long jump shots. It was a quarter so very rare in its excellence—and what made it special was that it came against one of the top teams in the league with one of the best centers around.

The Spurs, who went 8 for 23 and had 8 turnovers and only 6 rebounds, were just overwhelmed. I guess I kind of was, too. I just kind of stood back and watched like everybody else. I didn't do any coaching. I was in total amazement, in awe. I couldn't believe what we were doing. People called it a perfect quarter and I think it was close.

I thought coming into the season that San Antonio would be the team we'd have to beat. I thought the Lakers would be good because they added Sam Perkins and Terry Teagle, but this team with David Robinson in the middle, as young as they were with another year together—I thought they were really going to be something. And this was a big game for them because we had beaten them the year before in the playoffs, and we were still undefeated.

But I've never seen looks on a team's faces like they had in that first quarter. They had no idea what hit them. We made all the shots and defended them incredibly. This is one game where I really did think it was over after the first quarter—with a 31-point lead. But I shouldn't have relaxed because they got back within 14 at halftime, and then I knew we could be in trouble.

It was almost like what Muhammad Ali did to George Foreman with his rope-a-dope. We punched them for the whole first quarter and hit them so many times we just collapsed. We'd punched ourselves out. We had nothing left in the second quarter. But the good thing was we responded at the end and still ended up winning 117–103.

But I'll never forget that first quarter. Whenever I need a little lift, I will pull out that videotape. The thing I will remember most is that dazed look on their faces. I remember looking at David Robinson and he seemed to be asking himself, "What in the world has happened to us?"

November 27, 1990

Portland—The glow of the San Antonio game didn't carry over to the next game. We had won 11 in a row when Phoenix came to town, another team we had beaten in the playoffs the year before. I think the San Antonio game woke them up. They came into town really ready to play.

Clyde got kicked out of this game in the second quarter, and we trailed 67–51 at one time. Then we came back and went ahead in the third quarter, outscoring them 32–15 during one run. I couldn't believe how quickly we caught them. We were up by 4, but they got 5 straight points to end the third quarter, and then we had nothing left in the fourth quarter and they beat us 123–109.

Still, after winning 11 in a row and almost going through the entire first month of the season without a loss, I just couldn't feel too bad about losing one. We had gotten off to the start we wanted.

November 29, 1990

Portland—We finish off the month with a home game
against Minnesota, and I want to make sure we don't stum-
ble. They're the only one of the four new expansion teams
to have ever beaten us, and I don't want it to happen again.

Our game-day routine is the same throughout the season.
We have a rather unstructured shootaround in the morning
about eleven o'clock. I let them just shoot and talk for about
twenty to twenty-five minutes. We don't do any drills or
anything. Then we walk through on the floor what our
opponents will do, and we walk through some things we'd
like to think about offensively. Then we look at about ten
minutes of videotape of our opponents.

On game nights, I don't like having a lot of idle time at
the arena before the game. Some of our players arrive very
early and go out and shoot. Others don't; some of our players
normally don't like to shoot before the game. I think you
have to respect that. As long as they're ready, they can set
their own pregame routine.

I tell the players they have to be in the locker room by six
o'clock if they need to be taped, and otherwise six-fifteen
for a seven-thirty game. Sometimes we change that to six-
thirty. We usually bring the players who are out shooting
into the locker room at ten minutes to seven. If we haven't
played a team previously that season, such as this night
against Minnesota, I may start my meeting with them at
about five minutes to seven. Usually, it's about seven. I get
to the arena somewhere between six-fifteen and six-thirty.

Our coaching staff—John, Jack, and Dan Burke, our video
coordinator—has already talked in the morning, and we talk
again about the other team. John will have the scouting
report written up by the time I get there.

We put the highlight tape on the big-screen TV for the
players who want to look at it, and then we get together for
a short meeting. I like what Mike used to do and still do it:
I ask the players to talk about the individuals on the other
team. Terry, for instance, talked about Pooh Richardson, the

Minnesota point guard. Everyone pretty much gets a chance to talk about our opponent's personnel. When we get through discussing the individual players, I talk about their sets—the offensive things they run—and John does the same thing.

I try to give the team a few minutes to themselves, then they always go on the floor with eighteen minutes showing on the game clock, indicating time remaining prior to the blow-off before the national anthem. After the team leaves is probably the worst time for me.

I've formed a kind of ritual. I seldom wear my tie and coat to the game; I just bring them and wear a casual shirt. So I kill that time getting dressed. Bob Cook, our team physician, is usually in the locker room then, and we often sit around and suffer through his jokes. Sometimes there's a game on TV and we'll watch that. But it's really just idle time.

I try to stay in the locker room until there's just one minute left on the clock. I don't like to go out there five minutes before the game and just stand around and wait for the teams to finish warming up.

Our preparation time was well spent on this night. We jumped Minnesota early in the game and won 107–92 to complete the first month of the season with an incredible 12-1 record. We're just a month into the season, and we've already got a three-and-a-half game lead in the division.

December

December 1, 1990

Seattle—We opened the month with a game that took almost until December 2 to complete. This amazing game, like the Laker game, appeared for a while to be a lost cause.

First, though, we had the game won. We were up by 4 points with forty seconds to go, and we let them back in it. Then they took the lead by a point before Jerome was fouled at the buzzer. He makes both and we win it. But he missed the first one—he had been having trouble at the free-throw line—and the crowd was going nuts. But he showed a lot of character because he knocked the second one down to send it into overtime.

This was the craziest, most bizarre game. Xavier McDaniel and Jerome always go at it. In the overtime, McDaniel got called for a foul, then Jerome pushed Xavier, and the officials called a technical foul on Jerome. So they made a free throw to put them ahead 106–103 with two seconds to go.

We got the ball in to Terry Porter and he got fouled. They were trying to foul him because they had a foul to give. Even if they got him while he was shooting, they were willing to put him on the line for two free throws because that would give them the game. They fouled him before he shot, then they fouled him as he shot, but no foul was called.

The shot, from 3-point range, should have been no good. It came after the buzzer. But somehow the thing went in and they counted it. Being a typical coach I was really mad then because I thought they should have given him a free throw, too, and we would have won the game right there. I didn't want them to call the foul initially, but after he let the ball go, I wanted that foul bad.

So we go into the second overtime and find ourselves down again, this time by 4 with seven seconds to go. But Gary Payton made a bad decision on an inbounds play and fouled Danny Ainge. Payton had gone for a steal on the inbounds pass, fouled Danny, and hardly any time went off the clock. Danny makes two free throws and suddenly we're back in the game.

They call a time-out and take the ball out of bounds at halfcourt, and we switch on all their screens, so McDaniel tries to throw a crosscourt pass that Ainge tips away, making a great pass to Terry for a lay-up. We had tied it again and had it into a third overtime.

Incredible. We needed a free throw at the end of regulation, a 3-pointer at the end of the first overtime, and then 4 points in the final seven seconds of the second overtime.

Then we went right out and fell behind by 4 points in the third overtime. But we got right back and took the lead, and once we did, I knew we'd win the game and we did—130–124. If we had lost, it would have meant two losses in our last three games, and maybe we would start stumbling and going back and forth. But it turned out to be like the Laker game. We won it and it jump-started us again.

December 2, 1990

Portland—We had to come right back the next night at home and play Utah, and it may have been one of our most solid efforts of the year, coming right off the emotional win at Seattle the previous night. Karl Malone had 36 points in this game, but we played really tough the whole way. Buck really took it to Malone at the other end. Buck ended with 23 points and 11 rebounds, and we won 101–97.

We could easily have lost at Seattle, then come home and lost the Utah game, too. Instead, we're 14–1. We are setting a standard.

December 4, 1990

Miami—Our four-game road trip began with a win at Miami even though we didn't really play that well. Terry made some big shots down the stretch, and we escaped with a 98–95 win in an effort that was just enough. We feel good, though. We're 15–1 and are off to a good start not only on this road trip but on a difficult month of our schedule, which features two trips east and 12 of the 18 games on the road.

December 5, 1990

Orlando—Consecutive nights in Florida don't frighten you the way a swing through Texas can. The Magic just couldn't defend us; they have a really good offensive team, but for some reason they have trouble guarding us. We get a lot of easy baskets against them, and they have trouble with Clyde. He got 27 points and we won 119–110.

I don't care much for traveling anymore. I don't like being away from home and my family. That's also why I've tried to cut back on appearances when I'm at home.

When the team is at home, I don't want to be in the office

and I don't want to do a lot of appearances at night. Sometimes enough is enough. I'll do things during the day, like a luncheon or something. But these things just mount up. I'll get back home from practice and my message machine will have calls from writers in Houston, Long Beach, and Dallas. They all want me to call back right away. Then my local beat writers want me to call them back, too.

Suddenly, you're on the phone for an hour or two after you get home. It takes away from the quality time with your family. You have practices, a lot of videotape to look at, some meetings in the office—it all mounts up.

And at the same time, you want to be a father and a husband, too. A hard part of this job is that sometimes you get to the end of the day and you're real tired and you realize you haven't been a father—because you got home and didn't have any energy.

When I was an assistant, I just had no idea what this job involved. I have more sympathy now for Jack and Mike. When I was an assistant coach, the meetings and practices ended and I just went home. No one ever wanted to talk to me. I just did my thing and nobody really noticed. I never realized the demands on your time.

December 7, 1990

Indianapolis—This is a difficult place to play. They have a great offensive team, but we just killed them the whole game. We really played well and beat them 127–105. We jumped all over them in the first half, and Clyde really did a job on Reggie Miller.

The Pacers with Miller and Chuck Person have two of the most explosive players in the league. They also have one of the NBA's most versatile players in Detlef Schrempf. Their problem is their lack of an inside game.

When the Pacers are shooting well, they're deadly—very tough to beat. But when they aren't, you can really get out and run on them. If Rik Smits or someone else can give them a consistent inside game, they'll be a team to contend with. Until then, they'll tend to be inconsistent and will have a hard time beating the good teams.

Person loves to talk to his opponents, especially if he has his game going. Jerome will sometimes get into this a little, but he usually just goes out and plays that much harder. Talking trash should have no effect on a professional. You talk trash in this league and you'd better be a very good player or your life will become unbearable. Players in the NBA will make you pay.

We're 7–0 on the road after this game with a big test on the horizon—the Bulls in Chicago Stadium.

December 8, 1990

Chicago—Obviously this was a big game. We had just beaten Indiana on the road—a good team that was very explosive. But they weren't in the upper echelon of the league. There's a difference between winning a road game like that and going into Chicago, where it's more like a playoff game. You're not going to win there by 20 points. It's not going to be a blowout, and you know that before you arrive.

You'd think the league would have more respect for this matchup. First we play them at home the night after a game in Denver, and now we get them as a fourth road game in five nights. We play only two games a year against them, and they're both under circumstances that make it tough to play our best. It's frustrating.

We played a real solid game. We were up 13 points at halftime and won 109–101. We won against one of the better teams in the league, in their building, and after beating them at our place. It's tough to play there because it's so loud and Jordan plays so well. It's probably the most fun arena in the league to play in. The atmosphere is terrific.

I remember saying to somebody, Jordan's not going to beat us by himself. And that's what happened. He had a good game, but we made him work on defense and the other people didn't hurt us.

Jordan is the toughest player in the league to play against; Magic is also very tough, but I've felt in the last two years we are one of the few teams in the league that can really give them problems. We aren't like Detroit where we have this master defensive game plan against Jordan—this top-secret plan that nobody else has to slow him down. But we have Clyde and he challenges Jordan.

Clyde is his size, and what we have going for us that a lot of other teams don't have is that Jordan also has to play Clyde. Clyde really goes after him, and I think it takes away a little from Jordan when he has to play a guy so similar to himself. And it isn't like it is when he has to guard Magic; when he plays Clyde, he isn't playing defense just in the halfcourt. He has to play the full length of the court continually, and that's a little different for him.

I think one of the reasons Detroit has always done well against him—never mind that "Jordan rules" hype—is that he has to guard Joe Dumars, and Dumars has had big games against them.

We also have a good matchup with Scottie Pippen because we have Jerome. He's got to get out and run with Jerome or he's going to get hurt. Duck has always played well against them, too. He's from Chicago and always seems to come back and haunt them.

We've beaten them three of the last four times we've played them over the last two seasons. We didn't dominate them or humiliate them, but we beat them.

After this trip we're 8–0 on the road, and the thing I remember most is how well Terry played every night. He makes the big shots. It's incredible what he has done. I don't know if there is another guy who's reached all-star status at point guard who never played the position until he got in the pros. I mean, that just doesn't happen. Most guys who play point in the pros have been playing it pretty much all their lives. They may have been scorers in college, but they probably still had the ball in their hands all the time.

But for Terry to make the transition from being a forward

at a small college to becoming one of the top five point guards in our league is incredible. We have Jerome and Kevin Duckworth, who are also from small colleges, but Terry is a great example of a guy coming in who is, at first, just trying to make a team.

He was drafted, but he thought he would get drafted higher. We had two other point guards, Darnell Valentine and Steve Colter, but we took him with the last pick of the first round because you just couldn't pass him up. He was one of the top guards in the draft and was sitting there available. There wasn't a better player left, so we took him. He really didn't know if he was going to make the league, but he worked his tail off. I think his rookie year was disappointing for him, but by the all-star game he was playing better than the other guys and we traded Darnell.

I think most players—especially those from small schools—go through different stages. His first stage was just to make the league. Then he got a starting job, and when he did that, he had to prove that he was a legitimate starter. He was asked to lead then, but when you ask someone to lead who is still just fighting for status in the league, it really isn't fair.

You can't really ask him to lead, especially when you have such people as Clyde and Kiki Vandeweghe, who had been all-stars. We had a lot of guys who had been in the league a lot longer than he had. And a lot of guys kidded him a lot about being from Wisconsin–Stevens Point. So he hadn't made his mark yet and he wasn't comfortable leading then— even though he clearly had leadership qualities in him.

I felt at the time, Terry would never truly be the leader until one thing happened: he needed a contract that got him on equal footing with everybody else. It finally happened after the 1988–89 season. He played out his original contract and hit the jackpot. He made a heck of a deal. And the thing that impressed me the most is that the summer he got that contract was the summer during which he worked the hardest. He wanted to show he deserved the money.

After that contract, his level of play and his confidence

level—everything—was different. He was a different player. I think he finally felt accepted, that he had arrived—that he belonged. And I think the leadership role was a natural thing for him out on the court from that point on. In the playoffs last season he made big shots, rose to the occasion time after time. I saw a new maturity about him as a player and as a person. He knew he belonged with the top players in the league.

A lot of times you don't realize that he came from nowhere and it took him six years. But I think he's a much stronger person for it and a much better player because of it. He got there because of hard work, and he's never forgotten that.

Now it's just a matter of concentration for him. He knows he's good, and making the all-star team was one more stage for him. That he's an all-star now makes the story even more incredible. He's won so many games for us down the stretch. The only stage left for him is to be a champion.

On our trip, he was great down the stretch. Danny Ainge was telling people that Terry is "the most clutch player in the league." I don't think Danny realized how good Terry was until he got here and saw him play every day.

He'll never have the statistics of a Kevin Johnson or a John Stockton. Those guys don't have a guy like Clyde playing in the backcourt with them. That takes away from Terry's stats because he doesn't have the ball in his hands all the time like those guys do. We like Clyde to have the ball a lot, too. But whenever we need Terry, he's there. A lot of times at halftime we'll look at the stat sheet and he'll have taken only one or two shots and you have to tell him to look for his own shots more. Then, suddenly, he'll get 16 points in the third quarter and just open the game up.

There are more potent offensive point guards in the league right now than there are potent off-guards. I don't really know why, but a lot of good players are coming into our league now who are good offensive players and also great passers, guys like KJ, Stockton, Tim Hardaway, Terry. So the game has changed to go to them. More and more they are *the guy* on their teams.

Stockton is more like Terry except that he really looks for his assists more. He has the ball in his hands all the time. I mean, there's never a time he doesn't have it. Every play they run he has it. But he can score, too, when they need it.

Thank goodness I played back when I did. I could never play point guard now.

December 11, 1990

Portland—We came home from the trip to play Indiana again. They've been having some problems about this time. It looks as if Dick Versace is about to get fired. But they're just starting a road trip and we're just coming off one, and as a coach you always worry about that. It's a common problem in the league and we used to have it all the time, but not so far this season; we've come home and played some real strong games after road trips. I guess that's the maturity of our team. We get ourselves ready. This game was a good example—we just jumped all over them and were up 22 in the third quarter and won 122–96.

December 13, 1990

Sacramento—It's games like this that keep coaches humble and frustrated. It just happened, and like some of the wins we've had, it was hard to believe.

We came in with a 19–1 record, having won eight straight since our first loss. We absolutely dominated Sacramento twice during the exhibition season; they had a terrible time guarding us. I've always respected Dick Motta, but I didn't know he would come up with a defensive answer for us so quickly. One reason we don't ever seem to play well at Arco Arena is that we just don't seem to shoot well there. Even in our earlier regular-season game there, which we barely won, we shot poorly. The only thing I can think of to explain it is their baskets or their lights.

This was a strange game. We had played well at home and went down there and got ahead 38–19 at the end of the first period. We played a fantastic first period, and I thought we were just going to roll right through the game. But in the second quarter our second unit struggled on offense. We took a lot of bad shots, we didn't get back, we stopped defending them, and they got back into the game quickly. We're trying to cut back the minutes of our starters by using four or five bench players at the start of the second quarter, which is traditionally a substitute's quarter. It's the time to get your bench involved in the game, and up until now, they've done an outstanding job. But not tonight. I put the starters back in and it was as if we had forgotten how to play. We finally lost 100–88. Clyde went 1 for 9 in the second half of this one after going 1 for 16 in the first game there.

I told the team afterward that we were still 19–2 overall and 8–1 on the road. Teams in our league are going to lose to other teams—at home and on the road—that they don't expect to lose to. It's going to happen. The big thing is, you can't let it perpetuate itself. You can't worry about it. You just have to let it go, forget about it, and go on to the next game.

December 14, 1990

Portland—Even though we had eliminated them from the playoffs the season before in three straight games, Dallas always plays us tough. They control the tempo on us and keep the game close. We finally won a grinding game 106–104 and were lucky to win it. Terry hit a big 3 down the stretch and Cliff Robinson was very good.

Cliff has improved a great deal over last season. He's playing with more patience, his shot selection is much improved, and he's developing a much better overall game. Many times a player levels off or even drops off in his second year, but Cliff has steadily improved. I believe he can become one of the best defensive players in the NBA because of his size, agility, and quickness.

The Mavericks have been crippled by their problems with center Roy Tarpley, a talented big man who has had continual brushes with substance abuse. The Dallas franchise is a solid one with people who do their homework on the people they draft. They really cover themselves.

But this was a kid who, it was said, had his problems in college. You draft him and give him a couple of million dollars, and who can predict what he will do? He has a lot of money and a lot of time on his hands. Then he gets into trouble again and it's difficult to trade him because some teams don't want to take a chance on him. There's always a feeling, too, that you're going to be able to turn the guy around. Usually, by the time you realize you aren't, it's too late.

Our organization is pretty firm that with cases like Tarpley, you just don't take the chance. It just isn't worth it. Over the long haul, you're better off taking people who are solid than taking a chance on a guy trying to turn his life around. Usually they don't, but I hope Roy is able to overcome his problems.

December 16, 1990

Portland—With Orlando coming in you worry a little because of the way they can score. We were 18 points ahead of them in the third quarter and fell behind by 4 in the last quarter. Then we ended up winning by 19. It was another weird game, but Clyde always scores big against them. They don't have anyone to intimidate around the basket so we're able to finish a lot of plays. They remind me of our first Portland team because they try to outscore you. Still, it's better for us to play a team like this than one like Dallas, which controls the tempo. If you let us play a wide-open game, we play much better and generally shoot better.

December 18, 1990

Portland—When Golden State comes to town, you never quite know what to expect from their coach, Don Nelson. On this night he tried to slow the game down against us. It really surprised me. Nellie is always going to try something different against you; you can always count on that. His teams are smart, they understand what he wants to do, and they try not to give you what you want.

We always find it's better for us just to do quick-hitting things against them. We don't call our normal calls against them, either; we'll run another play, then step out and play pick-and-roll before they can adjust to it.

Our problem with them has always been on the defensive end. If we guard them, we usually win. If we're soft defensively, they're going to score and stay in the game with us. But they've never been able to defend us. Maybe for a half they'll do it, but we always break out. So it's a matter of who makes a defensive stand.

Nellie isn't afraid to change things for a game. He'll change style or personnel. He often plays small or big, and you have to try to figure out what he's doing. He has the reputation, and deservedly so, of being one of the best coaches in the NBA.

In this game Nellie had decided to walk the ball up the court in the first half to see if they couldn't stay close until the fourth period, when they would have a chance to win. It didn't work. We were ahead 30–6 at one point and 35–9 after the first quarter. I was really proud of our team because we saw what they were doing and our guys maintained their intensity on defense. The combination of our intensity and the fact that they were a little unsure about what they were doing—walking it up isn't their style—made it difficult for them. All of a sudden Mitch Richmond, Chris

Mullin, and Tim Hardaway were shooting standstill jumpers in a slow-paced game, and it threw their rhythm off. And every time they missed, we just ran the court. We scored 35 points in that first period despite their slowing it down. We led 70–38 at halftime and won easily, 122–94.

December 20, 1990

Oakland—We had to turn right around and go down to Golden State, and the Warriors beat us 125–118. They didn't hold the ball this time. They just ran. They jumped all over us and showed why they are such a scary team. Clyde kept us in the game, but Hardaway just killed us with 36 points and 15 assists. When their big three guys—Hardaway, Richmond, and Mullin—get it going, they can go into any building and win.

If they beat you in your building and then they go home, it's tough to beat them at their place. And Nellie does a good job. He prepares them well in this situation, which is more of a playoff-type setup.

Don Nelson is in a unique position. He's the only coach in the league who truly runs his team. I don't run the Trail Blazers, I just coach them. He coaches the Warriors and also runs the team. You don't do what he says, there's nobody to run and talk to. And his track record speaks for itself. They just beat us in this game, and the first thing I thought about after the game is what a scary playoff team they would be, especially in a short, five-game series with those three guys on a hot streak.

December 21, 1990

Los Angeles—We had to play the Clippers the night after losing to the Warriors. We didn't play well in the first half, but Terry came out in the second half and picked up Gary

Grant fullcourt, and that seemed to get everyone going defensively. We took them out of the game in the third quarter and cruised the rest of the way to a 117–107 win.

December 23, 1990

Portland—We came home and beat Denver 132–101, and the only thing memorable about the game is how cold it was in Memorial Coliseum. It was very cold outside and they told us the building just couldn't keep pace. It's funny, but they never heat it up for us, anyway. We had to cancel our shooting practice in the morning because it was just too cold. We went out, walked on the court, and just turned around and walked back into the locker room. Too cold. Our shoot-arounds have been deteriorating all year from the cold. We've complained about it several times, but it hasn't changed. I think they could have stored the unsold hot dogs at center court and they wouldn't have spoiled.

I've been battling a cold and sore throat for a week or so, and this only made it worse. Once you get a cold during an NBA winter you have a good chance of holding on to it for a long time.

December 25, 1990

Portland—It's Christmas, and under our tree we found a typical NBA gift—a trip to New York on Christmas Day. It's just ridiculous for a professional league such as ours to do things like this. I guess I can understand football doing something like this because they are in the middle of playoffs and they only have so many weeks to get them finished. If Christmas happens to fall on a Sunday, they have to play.

But here we are in the middle of an 82-game schedule—with twenty-seven teams in our league—and we have to go coast to coast on Christmas Day. It's ridiculous. Part of the problem is that for years we had to be out of town between Christmas and New Year's Day because of the college tournament, the Far West Classic, that was then played in Memorial Coliseum. But that tournament is dead now and we are still sent out on the road.

Anyway, here we are on a day that's a holiday for everyone in the country but us, traveling from Portland to New York. I don't understand it. It's amazing to me that the players' association hasn't made a stand on this. The league says you can't travel on Christmas Eve, but then on Christmas Day you can do whatever you want. So they schedule us to play New York the day after Christmas, then tell us we can't leave until three P.M. December 25. That means you're not going to get to New York until midnight or whatever. There's just no feeling for the people who have to do this.

Isiah Thomas and Bill Laimbeer chartered their own plane Christmas morning to get to Chicago. I don't blame them a bit. That way they got Christmas Eve at home with their families.

It's interesting to me that the Lakers-Bulls games can always be scheduled for Sunday afternoons to accommodate CBS and NBC; there's never any trouble doing that. You can always schedule those rivalries for Sunday afternoons, but you can't schedule us to play somebody like the Sonics or Warriors or Kings the day after Christmas? So we could fly in the morning of the twenty-sixth and spend Christmas with our families. Well, why not? Why do we have to play Eastern Conference teams this time of year?

And then of course it's always four games in five days. That's the other thing I really have a gripe with the league about. We go back east and always play four games in five days. When we go there, we lose three hours and we're always having to do that. But very few Eastern teams come out here and play four games in five days. I've hardly ever seen that. A lot of them have long trips out here, mostly because of scheduling conflicts in their arenas. That's why we played Chicago so early; they always have a long Western trip in November.

But we're always going to play four in five days after

Christmas because there are only five days until New Year's Day, since you're not supposed to play on New Year's Eve.

I was really tempted to try to fly to New York on the twenty-sixth, the day of the game. If we were late for the game, too bad. But it would have hurt the team, and our owner would have been subject to a fine if we missed the game. So we ended up going on Christmas, and the players weren't real happy about it. The league had no intelligent answer as to why we had to do this. And we weren't the only ones; Seattle had to do it, too.

We used to play on Christmas night in Portland and I hated it. The people in our front office always said, "It's a great night to play. Everyone is done with their Christmas by the evening, and it gives them something to do." That's nice for our fans, but it means we have to go to work. We have to prepare for the game.

So, anyway, we got on our plane on Christmas Day, and Ainge had brought T-shirts on board for everyone, with his own nicknames on them. There were some great nicknames. Wayne Cooper's said "Wrinkles" in deference to his status as the team's oldest player. Terry Porter's shirt had a couple of Spanish words that translated to "Big Balls," referring to Porter's courage at the end of games.

Then for Geoff Petrie, who negotiated those new contracts for Jerome, Clyde, and Buck over the summer, he brought a box of candy. Empty. He put a note in it for Geoff saying he intended to give him some candy, but that Jerome, Clyde, and Buck took it all. It was his good-natured way of pointing out that his contract needs to be redone, too.

Danny loves life. He just really enjoys what he's doing and enjoys everyone around him. There aren't a lot of people around like him. He never seems to let himself get down. We don't have a lot of personalities like him, and sometimes the guys just tell him to go sit down and shut up and leave them alone. But he usually gets them laughing, and he's always got people going.

He gets on guys something terrible. And they get on him. In shooting practices he'll get guys in shooting games or playing one-on-one. I remember one day he got Cliff Robinson going at one-on-one, and they went all out for twenty minutes. It got real competitive. He has a way of doing that. When the NCAA playoffs were going to start, he organized a whole playoff pool. Everybody picked teams and it was a lot of fun. We had never done that before.

He's added so much to our team. He's competitive and he's been around. He's experienced in winning and losing— and very opinionated about things. He really enjoys talking about the league, and that's another difference between this team and some past Blazer teams. These guys really talk a lot about the league and what's going on. They're very aware as a group. In the past, a lot of times they just didn't seem to care. They just played their games and went on. I think it's important and Danny's brought a lot of it to us.

Danny brought the Christmas presents not only for the players and coaches, but also for Mike Shimensky, our trainer, and he bought aprons for our flight attendants. It was a real nice touch to start the trip.

December 26, 1990

New York—We opened the trip in Madison Square Garden, and I never worry about playing in New York. There's so much media and we had played so well to that point, I was sure we'd be ready to play. I even canceled our shoot-around in the morning because I knew we'd be ready for this game.

Clyde and Terry love to play here. And in this game they were really good. Clyde was all over the place, getting 9 rebounds, 5 assists, 2 steals, 3 blocks, and 27 points. We won 108–92 and it was a great game for us.

You get up for the games in New York for obvious reasons. I think with us it's that the guys want to do well because we don't normally get much exposure. When we go there, there's so much media attention, and if we play well, they realize how good we are. I don't remember us ever playing poorly there. We just killed them in the second half, and Duck scored 24 points. We were 24–3 after this one.

Patrick Ewing, who is a great player, played very well against us. When he was in college, he was mainly a defender and rebounder. As happens so often in our league, he showed he could do far more than he did in college when he got to showcase his individual skills. Michael Jordan and Clyde Drexler are two great examples of this type of player. Their games took off because of the style of play in the NBA.

When we play the Knicks we don't worry about Ewing and how many points he scores. We try to shut down everyone else, especially in the first three quarters, and eliminate their easy opportunities. We want to make Patrick work for every shot. In the fourth quarter we may alter our strategy depending on our success to that point.

Ewing is a force at the offensive end and is becoming a much better passer each season. At the defensive end he's always a threat off his own man to block shots. We try to go right at him with Duck to keep him occupied.

He is a very good rebounder, but again, we take him away from the basket and force him to guard Duck. This limits his rebounding effectiveness. Also, by being the main threat of their offense, he has the ball a lot and that limits his chances to get to the offensive boards. As his team gets better, he will expand his all-around game.

We have always had success against the Knicks because they don't defend us very well and can't keep us out of the open court.

December 27, 1990

Charlotte—We had to play the Hornets the next night after winning at New York, and it was scary because they hadn't won a game through the entire month of December. The regular season's funny sometimes. You don't worry about playing the good teams, just the bad ones or the ones having a bad time. We just hung on all night and made some big

plays down the stretch. We seem to have developed the
ability to make the big plays and turn it up defensively in
the fourth quarter, and that's what we did to win 105–96.

December 29, 1990

Cleveland—We had a night off in Cleveland—great, huh?—
and then went out and beat the Cavaliers 120–114. It was
my one-hundredth win as a head coach in the NBA, but I
didn't know it until the writers asked me about it after the
game. I was a lot more concerned with Jerome after the
game, anyway.

He pulled a calf muscle and it really scared me because at
first I thought he had done something to his Achilles tendon.
He just stopped and kind of froze out on the court. That was
unusual because normally he would always try to move if
he could. They told us he'll be out for a couple of weeks
and that's going to be a problem.

You really don't know what he does for us on the floor
until you look at the videotape. I remember sitting down
once with Paul Allen and Bert Kolde and going over some
tape. It was a good session; they wanted to get a better idea
of what we were trying to do, and we spent three hours
going over it. And Jerome was just incredible on that tape.
I don't think they realized how good he really was.

He is a different kind of small forward—a unique player,
really. Usually small forwards are in the James Worthy,
Dominique Wilkins, Chris Mullin mold—scoring machines,
highly skilled players. Jerome has really made himself a
player through hard work and a high degree of competi-
tiveness. He was never satisfied just to make a team; he
wanted to be the best player he could possibly be. He actually
spent five years in summer leagues, working on his game.

He's not what you would call a shooter, but he has made
himself a decent shooter. He's really tough to guard, though,
because he's a relentless offensive rebounder and runs the
floor so well. He makes more effort plays than anyone in

the league. The only other small forward like him is Dennis Rodman. He's kind of like Rodman in that he specializes. Jerome is a specialist in offensive rebounds, defending people, running the floor, and effort plays—running down someone who looks like he's got a fastbreak lay-up, keeping the ball alive on the offensive glass, coming up with a loose ball out of a pack. He's just a unique player.

In the Cleveland game, we caught a break when Craig Ehlo was kicked out early for taking a punch at Duck. That was really funny. Sometimes Duck just doesn't know how big and strong he is. He does things and doesn't even realize it. Ehlo had set a backpick for Brad Daugherty on Duck, then Duck threw his arm back to fight through the pick. They only problem was, Ehlo's head was there. Lenny Wilkens, the Cleveland coach, was really upset, and I don't blame him because the officials didn't see that part of it.

But I really believe Kevin didn't intentionally do anything. He was just trying to get by the pick. But Ehlo got frustrated and responded by throwing a punch, which the officials saw. You throw a punch in our league and it's automatic—you're out of the game, whether it lands or not. I think Lenny was thinking Duck should have gone, too, but the officials didn't see that part of it. I don't think Ehlo was thinking too clearly, either. I was reminded of the old line: if Ehlo ever really punches Duck and Duck finds out about it, Ehlo's in deep trouble.

December 30, 1990

Milwaukee—We finish the trip, and the year, with a game against the Bucks, who are undefeated at home. It turned out to be a hell of a game and a frustrating one for us. It was an amazing shooting display, with both teams stepping up and making 3-point goal after 3-point goal. They had so many different guys making them, and they didn't miss a free throw until the final minute of the game.

We lost 117–112 but we didn't play poorly. We played

hard and pretty well for our fourth game in five nights. We didn't have Jerome, so I told Cliff before the game to be careful at the start, to be a little conservative and not pick up quick fouls. Then he got three fouls in the first four minutes of the game. That changed our rotation dramatically. I had to slide Clyde down to small forward for a good part of the game. Ricky Pierce was knocking down every 3 he saw, and Jay Humphries hit a big one near the end for them.

I was really frustrated after this game because we didn't get to the foul line very often and it seemed as if the Bucks were there every time we touched them. But you have to hand it to Milwaukee. We wanted to be the first team to beat them at home and they wouldn't let it happen.

But by this time I was really getting used to us winning on the road. It used to be that we went on the road and just hoped to win. Now we expect to win every game. Our confidence level is so high.

I think a lot of what goes into winning road games is experience. Our goal last season was to win twenty games on the road. But after another season together and winning games in some pretty rough spots, we've changed that goal. This season we want to have more road wins than any team in the league. We no longer look at winning on the road as something we can't do. We've been around long enough to know we can win on the road.

We're 27–4 and even though we just lost a half-game off our division lead, we're still seven games in front.

We've responded to all the challenges so far. We set the tone with our wins at home early and now we've won on the road, weathering a difficult travel month. I have a great sense of pride and even more faith in our players. To come out this season and play at this level is a tremendous accomplishment. All we have left is four months and fifty-one games.

January

January 3, 1991

Portland—We open the new year with the Lakers coming in for the first time this season. The Lakers' appearances in Portland the last two years have been to our fans, the most important games of the season. It's almost as if this one game means ten games. At least that's how the fans approach it.

I think this atmosphere hurts our guys a little. Everybody looks at it like, if you don't win this game, well, you haven't proved yourself. You're not the team everybody thinks you are. And let's face it, everybody who has been here a while has gone through a lot of losses to the Lakers, and a lot of games when you feel as if you've made up some ground and gotten closer to them—and then they come in here and beat you. It was that way for so many years. You felt that whenever they came up here, they could just turn it up and beat you.

So much hype has been connected with the games up here. And it hasn't been just the fans, either. I shouldn't say it's just the fans. Our office, our own team, does it, too.

We've tried to downplay it among ourselves. We know we're a better team than they are. We know that our record speaks for itself. I've talked to the players about this; I told them if we don't beat the Lakers, it's not going to be the end of the world. A lot more games are left in the season. And if we beat them and then lose our next three games, what difference does it make that we beat them?

I tried to take some of the pressure off our team, but this game just wasn't meant to be for us. The Lakers played a really solid game and beat us 108–104, slicing our lead from seven games down to six. We had just come back from that Christmas trip, we hadn't played in four days, and we just didn't play well the whole game.

Around town our record of 27–5 suddenly doesn't seem to mean much. We've lost two in a row and it's like, "What happened? Where are we going?" We lose a very tough game at Milwaukee, then lose to the Lakers at home. It happens. We have to put it behind us and move on. A lot of other games are to come.

The situation with the fans and the media in Oregon is unique. The Blazers had so many problems winning in the playoffs since the 1976–77 championship. Then when we hit it big in the playoffs and got to the Finals, nobody was prepared for the reaction. It just took over the whole state. It was incredible how it took over. The number of people who followed the team was amazing. Suddenly we were recognized everywhere we went. I guess I didn't realize the exposure the head coach gets because as an assistant it wasn't that big a deal. But it changed our lives completely.

After being in the Finals, there was absolutely nowhere we could go. We went to Hawaii for our twentieth anniversary and went into a restaurant and someone said, "Aren't you the Portland coach?" I was swimming in the ocean and someone recognized me. I never expected that. I never dreamed it could happen. So many games are on cable TV and the networks, once you go somewhere in the playoffs everyone gets to know your face.

It's hard. It's difficult for our whole family. People are

well-meaning, but you just can't go anywhere. People stop you and ask you things or want to talk about the team, and your own kids just stand there waiting for you to get through with it. Your kids don't want that exposure.

My children have been tremendous and so has Mary Kay. I'm sure it hasn't been easy for the kids at school. The identity they have there is not theirs, it's mine—actually it's not even mine, it's just the job I have.

I have to admit that no matter what I say, it's changed me. I've been shorter with people, I'm sure. You just get so tired of it. I've been short with people in our front office. I know I've been different from last year. It's just that sometimes you'd like to go and do something without having the job always there.

I enjoy the success. I enjoy the winning and enjoy the team. I've got a great job. But I don't think anyone understands what it's like and the crazy things that sometimes happen.

One time I was opening the door to the rest room at a theater and some lady grabbed my arm and pulled me back. She wanted an autograph. One time I was standing at a urinal in a theater and a guy walked up to me and asked for an autograph. I asked him, could you wait a minute? There are limits to things. Sometimes people don't understand that.

And in Portland the people are super. It's just that they're so caught up with the team. They just hope the team does well. They hope you do well. So I try hard to keep that in perspective.

Sometimes that's hard, too. Other things are going on in my life besides the Trail Blazers. I may be thinking about something that doesn't have anything to do with basketball when somebody comes up. Then I don't respond the way they would like and they get ticked off. It doesn't have anything to do with them; I just have trouble with always being "on."

I think it's all worth it, though, because I'm doing what I've always wanted to do. The rest of it comes with the territory, and if you can't accept that or live with it, you'd better go back to a lower-profile job. But I wish everyone could understand what it's like.

It can be tough on the kids and Mary Kay. I go on the road; she doesn't. She has to deal with it the whole time, and it seems as if everyone knows who she is. She can't get away from it.

I get to deal with the good things and then get out of town on a road trip. Often if someone wants something out of me, such as an autographed ball, she has to deal with these people; they don't want to bother me, so they call her. She's a very approachable person and is happy to help whenever she can. But it's not her career, and on top of it she has to deal with me and my mood swings. She's basically a private person, but because of my job she has lost a lot of her privacy.

She has five basketball schedules this year—the kids' and mine. It's difficult to coordinate it all.

I love going to watch the kids play, but when I do, I try to go up in the bleachers and sit in the corner. I just want to watch the game; it's their time and I want to give them my full attention. But I don't know how many times I've had somebody come up during one of their games and say, "I bet you don't get to do this very much." You just sit there and try to watch your child play, and they sit for a half hour and talk to you about the Blazers. You can't really ask them to leave you alone without causing hard feelings, so you're stuck. Mary Kay goes through the same thing.

I don't want to sound as if I am complaining, because I'm not. I'm just trying to give you a picture of what it's like. Just imagine you had a job that you're reminded of constantly, every minute of the day. That's what weekends are supposed to be for—to get away from your job. But we don't have any weekends.

It's hard on the kids, too. Kathy, twenty, is playing basketball at the University of Portland, and R.J., eighteen, played at Tigard High School last year. They both have been very successful. What they've done has nothing to do with the fact that I'm coaching the Trail Blazers. And I don't think they like the attention. They just want to be normal kids and go about their business. But they've handled it all well. They do well in school and they have good friends. They've handled it very well.

Laura is fifteen and David is ten, and they're excited. They're young enough that for them it's a lot of fun. But as you become a teenager, I don't think you want a lot of attention drawn to yourself, especially when it has nothing to do with who you are and what you're doing. It puts undue pressure on you.

The other thing that's hard on the family is that they hear things at home about the team, because I talk with them about it. They know more about our team than most people, but they can't talk about it. The kids hear things around the house about whom we might take in the draft or possible free agents we're interested in. Sometimes, I might even mention a trade; when we were going to make the trade for Buck, they heard me discussing it on the phone at home. It's tough for a kid to keep a secret like that when the Blazers are so important to everyone they know. But to the best of my knowledge, they've always kept everything to themselves.

January 5, 1991

Portland—We beat Miami 132–111 and had no problems. But I still can't get rid of that cold that started in mid-December. It's just hanging on.

January 6, 1991

Portland—Seattle came in the next night and gave us all we could handle. We jumped off to a big lead, and then the Sonics made a run right back at us. We were 24 points ahead in the second quarter, but they came back and took the lead in the fourth quarter.

With three minutes to play I had three guards on the floor. That was our best offensive group that night, and it matched up pretty well defensively. Danny Ainge had taken two bad shots, 3-pointers, and one was even an airball. We were down. Danny walked over to Clyde and said something to him. The next time down the court, Clyde penetrated and kicked it out to Danny, and he knocked down a 3. Right after that, on the next possession, we were down by 2 and swung the ball back to Danny, and he hit another 3 to put us up by a point. We hung on for dear life and got the win. I found out later that Danny went over to Clyde—they were really running at Clyde, double-teaming him—and told him, "I'm going to make the next one." He had just shot an airball. After that, a lot of guys would just want to run away and hide. He says, keep coming to me, I'm going to make the next one. We got to him, he makes two huge 3s, and we win the game 114–111.

We executed well at the end of the game, with Clyde hitting Terry off our 2-out play for a wide-open lay-up that pushed us in front in the final minute. That was important because I know that if we're going to win a championship, our ability to execute down the stretch is going to be what wins for us. Everybody has to understand that.

At the end of games you want to give yourself a chance to take whatever the defense is going to give you. You can't say, okay, this is what we're going to do—and if it doesn't work, it's over. That's why I say, okay, about four or five things can happen for us with this play that are good.

On that particular play, which we've used successfully many times so far, Terry can get a lay-up right away. Or we can post Terry against a smaller point guard. Or Clyde can penetrate or play pick-and-roll with Duck to get Duck open for a jump shot. Clyde can go to the hole if it's there, then we have Terry coming off a double pick for a shot. A lot of good things can happen off that play. And Clyde usually does a good job of deciding what to do with the ball.

We're fortunate that Duck shoots so well. Our pick-and-roll is such a good play because of his ability to shoot the ball from the outside. Even if he's not playing well, the defense has to honor him. He beat Phoenix in the playoffs last year with a jump shot from the baseline even though he hadn't been playing well the whole game. If you leave him open, he's going to make the shot. It gives us such a threat down the stretch of a game.

I try not to use some of our best plays in the first half. I'll run a few pick-and-rolls to see how the defense is going to play them, but will usually just use quick-hitting things to see how the defense will rotate. The only time you'll see us run something like our "2-out" play in the first half is if we're really struggling, the other team's on a run, and we need a basket badly.

If you run your bread-and-butter plays too much, they can lock in on them. But I don't care if they cover them in their shootaround and talk about them for years: after thirty-six or forty minutes of a game, if you suddenly start running a play, it's going to look new and they're going to have to make some quick judgments on the floor. So it doesn't make any sense to run that type of play until you need it. We have about four or five that we won't run unless we really need a basket and it comes down to the end.

We work on them a lot in practice, but our game isn't based on set plays. We're so much better when teams can't lock in on us. When we've had trouble in the past, it's been when we started standing around, and that's why I've gone to more of a passing game and just let them play—we're just a better team that way.

We can run things if we need to, but it's not good for us to run plays continually. We get stagnant. And we're really not a great shooting team. It's as simple as that.

January 8, 1991

Houston—We caught Houston in its second game after Akeem Olajuwon went out with his eye injury. They were in disarray this game and we played well. We dominated them. They got behind and just didn't compete and we beat them 123–97.

I think this game may wake them up a little—or break them down. They lost to us by 26 points at home. Games like that at home have an effect on teams.

January 9, 1991

Dallas—The Mavericks hammered us 109–99. Duck got thrown out of this game and Clyde got into it with Jake O'Donnell. There's been a problem between some of our players and Jake for a while. It's obvious. Jake has tried to distance himself from us totally and not say a word to anybody on our team. He knows there is a problem. This kind of thing happens in this league frequently. Jake's one of the top-rated officials in basketball, and for whatever reason, we seem to have a problem with him. All teams and all officials go through this at times.

When he doesn't talk to you, though, you feel that he thinks he's above it all—that we have no right to talk to him. That's how Jake makes me feel.

When the official at least acknowledges that you have a stake in the game, you can get along with him. Sure, you're going to get upset at them, but it always seems to our team that Jake nails us more than some other people. I think that's what's bothering our players. But it's a two-way street and we've had to learn some things, too.

The guys I really respect and like are the ones who acknowledge you if you have a question. I'm sure a lot of them say I gripe a lot, but I like to be talked to like a human being. I think the league makes a big mistake in saying that we're out there for a hundred games a year with those officials and that we're not supposed to have any kind of a relationship with those guys.

A guy isn't going to play favorites just because he talks to a coach. Sometimes they act as if you can't talk to them, can't say hi, can't shake hands or be cordial. They don't want you to be a human being with them. Well, that's ridiculous. It's an emotional game. And the officials have so much of an impact on the game. I mean, their calls can cost me my job. It's just ridiculous to think I'm not going to react to their calls. If you have some kind of a feeling for what type of person a ref is, you're less likely to jump all over him and explode. And you're more likely to explode if they act as if you're the dirt of the world.

You have to learn, though, to temper yourself and learn what each official likes and what he doesn't like. For instance, I like having Hugh Evans in a game because before he'll give me a technical he'll tell me, "If you don't relax, I'm going to give you a technical." When I hear that, I ease off. I know I've gone too far. Earl Strom, who's now retired, was much the same way.

But some guys will just nail you and say, forget you. I think there's an inconsistency in that, because they don't do that with every coach, just some of them.

And if you have a problem with an official in one game, it should be over when the game's over. I've had problems with such guys as Mike Mathis, Hugh Evans, and Ed Rush, guys who were around even back when I played; they've been pretty upset with me, but then the next time I see them, it's forgotten. They're professional about it and it's my job to be professional about them in the same way. But with some officials, that isn't the case. I have a hard time with that, but I think it comes from someone telling a lot of the young guys especially that they have to be hard-nosed.

There's also an attitude toward assistant coaches in this league that I don't like. When I was an assistant, they had a rule that the assistant coaches couldn't get off the bench. I mean, give me a break. They're working, too. They're going to react. It's an emotional game. But assistants aren't supposed to talk to the officials or show any emotion on the bench. It's like, "No, you can't talk to me, you're only an assistant coach."

The league's side of it is that they can't have three guys there yelling at the officials, and I agree with that. But there

are ways to say, "Hey, I can't listen to all of you. Be quiet."
Acting as if assistants don't belong or don't have a stake in
the game is ridiculous.

The officials can take money out of your pocket. They can
get you fined. (They say the officials are fined, too, but I
don't know. Everybody knows when a coach or a player
gets a technical or gets fined, but nobody knows anything
about officials getting fined.) They can give you a technical
anytime they want. And it just cracks me up. All they put
down is "unsportmanslike conduct" on the report. It blows
me away. They don't ever put in the report what I did, just
"unsportsmanlike conduct." They should have to say what,
exactly, I did to cost myself $100. Then I could deny I did
it. But they can give me a technical because I looked sideways
at somebody.

Unsportsmanlike conduct. One hundred bucks.

I think it's really unfair. I got one where I reacted to a
foul on Jerome that was his third of the game. I put my
hands in the air and turned around to get Cliff into the game
for Jerome, and the next thing I knew, I had a technical. I
got the report and there it was—unsportsmanlike conduct.
Was it unsportsmanlike to put my hands in the air, or to
turn around and find another player to put in the game?
Whatever I did that caused it, put it in the report and I'll try
not to do it again.

They use technical fouls indiscriminately. If they made a
bad call, they give you a technical because they're embarrassed and it's supposed to be okay and you're supposed to
accept that. You have no recourse. Rod Thorn in the NBA
office is tremendous at listening to us; you call Rod and he
listens. He will even look at videotape and tell me his version
of what happened. If he feels it's unfair, sometimes he'll
even rescind a fine. But the fact is, they still gave you the
technical and it affected the game and there's nothing you
can do about that. I just hope that the officials are looked
at, too.

Some of them will even admit mistakes, and when they
do, I back off right away. I can accept that they make mistakes; what I can't accept is the guys who'll never admit to

one. I wouldn't officiate for anything in the world; it's got to be the toughest job in the world. I think it's been tough, too, in the league because they added so many new ones all at once when they put a third man on the crews. You put a veteran official on a crew with another guy who's been in for a few years and then add a totally new guy. That must be a hell of a game to try to officiate with our rules and the illegal defense. What do you call? What don't you call? It's a tough thing to learn for a new guy. It takes time to understand our league and the players and then be consistent with your calls.

I try to be understanding about it. I just wish they'd remember that they're human and try to treat us as if we are, too.

January 11, 1991

Detroit—As always in this league, you have to put the losses behind you quickly. Ahead was another trip into the Palace and a bout with the Pistons. We had been looking forward to this game. It was a chance to show that our win here last year in the playoffs was no fluke.

It was a dilly of a game. We led them a good part of the night and should have won it, but we lost 100–98 in overtime. Isiah Thomas ran over the top of Buck on the way to the basket down the stretch, and the officials just ignored it. It was late in the game and it was a very big play.

This game was officiated with Detroit's reputation in mind. I felt that so strongly. I don't care what anyone says, Dennis Rodman does everything but throw Cliff Robinson to the ground, trying to guard him in the low post. And some of the stuff they did to Duck in the low post was incredible. But there were no calls. If we were allowed to do that, it would be a much easier game. But they're allowed to do a lot of things defensively that other teams aren't allowed to do because they've supposedly established it as their "style." If they get down by 15 points and they want to turn it up defensively and put their hands all over you and be very physical with you, that's supposed to be championship basketball.

Clyde goes into the low post and they push him and shove him and have their hands all over him, but because he's six foot seven and the guy guarding him is six three, it's okay to do that. But the fact that Clyde's bigger is an advantage we have, and it shouldn't be taken away from us just because their guy can't guard him within the rules.

When Buck stepped in on Isiah late in that game, everybody in the building thought it was a charge. But there was no call.

Also, I probably made some coaching mistakes.

Danny Ainge really had it going in the fourth quarter, and we didn't give him the ball. That's the problem we have sometimes because we're not used to having a shooter. To get guys their shots we run pick-and-rolls and put the ball in their hands. We're not used to having a shooter like Danny, and sometimes he doesn't get picks the way he should. Danny had it going, but we didn't get him the ball for about seven or eight minutes.

It was a great game and Detroit deserves a lot of credit; Isiah got Laimbeer the ball on a great pass and a great cut for the winning shot. That's what makes them so tough. They defend you down the stretch and execute late in the game.

But I think we felt good about this game because we played well enough to win, and with the way Danny played, we all know we're a better team than we were when we played them in the playoffs last year. It was a great game, win or lose, and it's fun when you have those kinds of games during the regular season.

It was a lot like our win in Chicago Stadium earlier in the season. It wasn't a typical regular-season game. It was knock-down-drag-out. You really have to persevere in a game like this. That's the difference between us now and us three years ago. We would never have persevered in this type of game. We would have lost this game by 15 points. We had won some games on the road and we would have just mailed this one in. We wouldn't have laid it all on the line.

Now we expect to win every game. I think all our guys and our coaching staff feel it. We're disappointed if we don't win. That's the most important thing you can accomplish as a coach; winning causes that feeling, and winning also flows out of it. Whatever happens this season, there's a real satisfaction in knowing we've achieved that point as a team. Now all we have to do is go out and do it.

January 13, 1991

East Rutherford, New Jersey—We're in the Meadowlands to play the Nets, and all everyone was doing was raving about their rookie power forward out of Syracuse, Derrick Coleman. We were giving Buck a pretty bad time about New Jersey finally having a power forward it could rely on. We rode him all day about how excited they were about getting this six-foot-seven, 225-pound power forward.

Then Buck went out there that night and just tore this kid apart. By the fourth quarter the kid was shooting 3-pointers and 20-footers because he couldn't even get a shot up anywhere near the basket. And he couldn't guard Buck. Buck just went right around him. We expected that going into the game; we watched the films and felt Coleman just didn't make much of an effort at that yet. I'm sure he will eventually, but right now he just allows people to post up. Buck really took it to him and we won easily, 116–103.

After the game I saw Danny Ainge standing there with a big smile on his face and I knew he had something to say. Finally he got the reporters' attention away from Williams's locker and said, "I was out here in the fourth quarter looking for a pay telephone. You know those child abuse spots Buck does on television? I was looking to dial that hot-line number."

And Buck did give the kid a whipping. Buck was 8 for 12

from the floor, 8 for 9 from the foul line, had 24 points, 10 rebounds, 3 steals, and a blocked shot. Coleman had 13 points but needed 16 shots to get them. He had 4 turnovers and fouled out.

January 14, 1991

Minneapolis— We got into Minnesota for a day off before playing the Timberwolves, and our assistant coaches, John Wetzel and Jack Schalow, and I got together with Geoff Petrie and began talking about picking someone up. Jerome has been hurt for a while, and we just felt we have to pick somebody up.

Some teams are interested in Drazen. New Jersey has been the one team most interested in him all year, but they don't have anyone we much want, and I wasn't interested in getting a first-round pick for him unless they'll give us their lottery pick. But they won't, and I don't blame them.

If someone gets hurt in the backcourt, Drazen can step in and play, but we'd rather get a quality player who can also play some small forward. It would make us stronger for the playoffs.

We have a lot of names. Ron Anderson's name was thrown around, because Philadelphia is interested in getting Adrian Dantley. But he's the only shooter they have coming off the bench, and I really can't imagine them trading him. But his name is out there.

Walter Davis is being talked about by Chicago, San Antonio, and the Lakers—all contending teams. Denver has made it known they're willing to trade him.

Dantley is still out there as a free agent and has expressed interest in coming to us and a couple of other teams. Geoff had some talks with his agent. It wasn't a monetary question, because he's pretty much willing to accept what we offered. But the big thing to me is how well he would fit into the team. The way we play, with great player movement and ball movement, well, he's a great offensive player, but when he gets the ball, you have to spot up and give him room. We're still not a great outside shooting team, and his presence might stop the way we play. So I'm concerned about whether he would fit in, basketballwise. Also, how would he fit in on the team if he didn't play a lot? He says that he could accept it. He feels if we play Detroit in the Finals again that he would really give us an edge because they don't like him and they're scared of him. That may or may not be true.

I felt all along—and I felt this strongly—that we're all in this together, the coaching staff, management, and the players. It's the players' team, too. I made it clear to the players that they weren't going to make the trade, but I did want them to have input. They knew who would fit in; they had played with and against all these guys.

I got the guys together in Minnesota who had been in the league for a while, and the starters. I couldn't get hold of Duck, so he wasn't in on it, but I talked to Terry and Clyde and Jerome and Buck about the different people we were discussing. I told them I wasn't interested in trading Drazen unless it was going to improve our team. I tried to be as honest with them as I could. I valued what they thought about the various players. I also told them I'd make the final decision on it, but I wanted to know what they thought.

We had a good meeting and they were very honest. We also talked about Dell Curry and Kelly Tripucka, who were also out there. We talked about all of them.

The consensus of the guys was that Walter was the best, and their reason was much the same as ours—that he'd also played some small forward. He isn't a true small forward, but he's played it some. He's a great outside shooter, obviously. Everyone felt his personality would fit in. And they all felt he would fit in with the style of game we play.

And let's face it—the players didn't think about it much but I brought it up—we didn't want San Antonio or the Lakers or Chicago to get him. That wasn't the reason we eventually got him; we got him because we thought he would help us. But I looked ahead at some of the teams in our conference, and I thought, if we play Golden State in the playoffs, he can play small forward against them. He can play it against San Antonio, Phoenix, and Utah, too. Some teams have very tall small forwards—the Lakers, for instance, when they use either Sam Perkins or James Worthy there. Walter would have a tough time at small forward against those kinds of teams. And we already have Clyde and Danny Ainge at off-guard. But he'd give our second team another shooter. He'd make us stronger.

They all agreed on Walter, but I didn't tell them whom I was leaning toward at all. I think if you don't ask the players when you're as close to a championship as we are, you risk damaging your team's chemistry. You have to have a feel for what the guys think.

It was a delicate situation because Drazen was still their teammate. I had told Drazen all along that people were interested in him but I was not going to deal him for a draft choice. Draft choices are great for the player personnel director and for the general manager: you get a ton of draft choices and all that does is help the next coach. It doesn't help me at all. It doesn't help us win a championship. Unless it's a lottery pick they want to give us, I'm not interested in any draft picks.

January 15, 1991

Minneapolis—We finally got around to playing the game and it was an interesting one.

Duck got sick and didn't suit up, and Jerome told me in the morning that he wouldn't be able to play because of his pulled calf muscle. But then just before the game he said if I needed him, he would play. Two minutes into the game, Buck went up for a shot and came down—and the next thing I know he's on his way off the court and into the locker room. He pulled a muscle or something and he just disappeared.

So I turned to Jerome and said, "You say you want to try it?"

He said, "Yeah." We were really shorthanded up front

and he said he'd give it a try. He played great. Mark Bryant came in and played a great game. He was posting up, taking his shot, and got really aggressive. He has a nice little turn-around jump shot that he used in college, but for some reason he had a hard time figuring out how to get it off in the pros. But he was great in this game. I played him almost the entire second half and we won 132–117.

We arrived back home late at night, and as usual, several people were at the Hillsboro airport, standing there with signs to greet us. I don't think there has been a trip all season when there haven't been fans there to meet our plane—no matter what time we arrived.

The people are just so enthusiastic about the team. It's part of their life. They go up and down emotionally with us. It's a good feeling, but sometimes it's a little bit disconcerting.

This might sound strange, but sometimes when things are going so well it's good to have a tough stretch—a kind of wake-up call—to make you realize it isn't always going to be easy. I don't mind a little wake-up call, but I don't want it to last too long.

Many times a player, a coach, or a team can get a false sense of security from success. Complacency can set in and you get to feeling that everything is going to be easy. When a tough time hits, though, people become much more receptive to what it takes to succeed. Our team always responds to adversity. We go back to the basic things that make us a good team—our defense and rebounding. This road trip has been one of those times. I think we'll come back strong.

January 18, 1991

Portland—We're finally home from a rough six-game trip. In a similar situation last year we came home and Washington beat us, but this time we beat them 123–99. We came out strong in the first quarter and were so good defensively.

I mean, every time Bernard King put it on the floor, we had two or three guys surrounding him. And that's hard to do to them because of their passing game. You usually can't lock your defense in. But all of our guys were so aware of helping Jerome and Cliff on him, and those guys did a great job. We just dominated them defensively the whole game.

January 20, 1991

Portland—We've got Milwaukee at home and it turned out to be another of those games where we jumped out big, 36–18, after the first quarter, and they came all the way back and went ahead by 10 in the fourth quarter. But Terry was good and we hung on and won 116–112 without Buck, who was still resting the injury he suffered against Minnesota.

We're beginning to make a habit of blowing leads. But I guess you can't blow big leads unless you get them, and you don't get big leads in this league unless you're playing pretty well. I'm not worried about it. This happens in the NBA to everybody. With our team it might happen a little more than with other teams, because we tend to play in spurts. What worries me is that we become impatient when we begin to struggle. Instead of making sure we execute when we need a basket, we try to jam the play down our opponent's throat. We're still maturing as a team.

January 22, 1991

Portland—Phoenix is in next and Buck still isn't playing yet. They beat us on the first game at Portland and played real well in this one. Jerome and Xavier McDaniel got into another one of their scraps and were thrown out in the third quarter. We had a 13-point lead in the third and fell behind in the fourth before pulling it out 123–116.

This was a key game for us because they were trying to make a statement against us. I do think if they had won this game, they would have had a psychological edge over us. So it was big for us to come back and beat them.

I had told Drazen that if we got close to making any trade for him, I would let him know. Before this game I told him that we were close to a three-way deal with New Jersey, but not to tell anyone because it wasn't over yet and anything could happen. Denver could still have called it off if they got a better offer for Walter Davis. Don't assume it's over yet; I told him that clearly.

Then the game ends and he's cleaning out his locker. He's upset. He's crying. And then I begin to wonder what I'm going to do if it all falls through at this point. I would have had to deal with him again, mend the fences again and all that stuff. Fortunately, it went through, and I honestly feel it was the best thing for everybody concerned. He went to a place where they wanted him badly. He's going to play. They had been after him all year.

So we sent Drazen to New Jersey, they sent a conditional first-round pick (not their lottery pick) to Denver, and we got Walter Davis. Walter indicated to me that he could accept his situation with us. I hope our fans will be as sensible. He's not going to come right in and break into the rotation. It's going to take me time to try to figure out how to use him. If I play him twenty minutes, then I change Danny Ainge's role and Cliff's role. I have to deal with twelve guys, not just Walter Davis. I don't feel we need him to win in the regular season, but he could make a difference in the playoffs. But it's not easy to get that point across to the public. I'm going to have to work him in, and I'm sure I'll hear about it on the talk shows.

We're six games ahead in the Pacific Division after beating the Suns, who are a very tough team. I'd put them on the same level as the Lakers and San Antonio, with Utah a notch below.

Offensively, there isn't a tougher team in the NBA. And now they've added Xavier McDaniel, who should give them a little more physical toughness. Phoenix has had a lot of injuries to key players, but they're going to be a team to be reckoned with by the end of the season.

The Suns present tremendous problems for us. Kevin Johnson is very hard to guard and when he gets it going from the outside, it's almost impossible. We want the whole team aware of him when he brings the ball up; he isn't just Terry Porter's responsibility.

The play that makes them the toughest is their pick-and-roll, with K.J. and Tom Chambers. It's effective for the same reason ours is hard to defend: Chambers slides to the wing and you can't get to him. And K.J. is often just too quick to double-team. Chambers can post up smaller people and take bigger people outside, where he can shoot or drive to the basket. Buck does a good job on Chambers, though, because he forces him outside and makes him work for every shot.

Jeff Hornacek is great for their team because he spots up and is a deadly shooter if you leave him to help on Chambers or K.J. He's also able to play point guard when K.J. comes out of the game. Dan Majerle and Mark West are great offensive rebounders and role players. And now the X-man gives them another scorer from inside and out, along with another rebounder.

They're a tough team because they're so good offensively. The key to their success will be how well they play defense.

January 26, 1991

Portland—The guys received Walter in a positive way, and I think it's going to work out well. He played his first game tonight against Sacramento, and we won 121–96. We killed them and Walter played thirteen minutes, scoring 6 points.

January 28, 1991

Portland—Atlanta is coming in next, and they're on a roll that got started when Bobby Weiss benched Moses Malone. They really came at us but we won by 5. It was a strange trip for them because they were playing really well and couldn't win. But they were very good against us, and we had to hit nine 3-point goals to beat them. That's a lot of outside shots.

January 31, 1991

Salt Lake City—We finished off the month by getting blasted by the Utah Jazz again. We played awful for the whole game. We shot poorly, defended poorly. Terry got hurt in the first quarter and never came back. It was just an awful game. I tried everybody on Karl Malone and he fouled everyone out.

We lost 105–91, but at least the word on Terry after the game was that his ankle sprain was not serious. We seldom seem to beat the Jazz in the Salt Palace.

february

February 1, 1991

Portland—We opened the month against Golden State, and Terry, suffering from an ankle sprain, couldn't play. But when Nellie went with his small lineup, I kept Duck in the game anyway, and they couldn't guard him. We won 119–99.

It's a hard decision because if Duck's not aggressive offensively—and he's not willing to pass the ball sometimes—it's hard to keep him out there when they go with the small lineup. It's not as much of a problem defensively because they usually have someone on the floor he can stay with, but offensively he has to take advantage. He's got to hurt them on the boards and he has to play smart. In this game he was really smart and we ended up forcing them to come back in with a big lineup to match up against him.

You treat every player differently and they all have their own way of doing things. That's all part of coaching. The thing about Duck is that he's often the biggest guy on the court, and when he makes mistakes, everybody is going to know about it. Duck's biggest problem is that he wants so badly to succeed that he really shows his emotions on the floor. He gets upset and very down. Everybody sees that.

He is trying like heck to make a change there. But nobody makes a change in his personality easily. It's even tougher in the kind of public lives we lead. Everybody else can change his personality or lifestyle in front of his wife or family. Duck has to do it out in public, in front of a lot of people who like to make fun of him. He's out there for everybody to see.

You don't have to motivate him at all—he works hard. You just have to keep him on track. You have to remind him constantly that he isn't ever going to be perfect. No matter what happens, he's still a key part of our offense. He sometimes doesn't realize that even when he isn't making shots, he's still helping our offense because of the kind of threat he is. We can run a post-up or a pick-and-roll for him, and if he rolls to the basket, they have to cover him. They'll sometimes run across the key to cover him and leave someone else open because they respect his ability to score.

He isn't a good passer, but I can't remember many big guys who came into our league and were good passers. Kevin McHale comes to mind as a big man who could pass the ball. Most big men who are good offensive centers are "go-to" people who do your scoring, not people you run an offense through. So they have to develop this skill. But Duck is getting better.

February 4, 1991

Portland—New Jersey came into Portland and it marked the return of Petro to Memorial Coliseum in a Nets uniform. He didn't play a good game and he drew a technical foul. We won the game 117–102.

I'm not so sure about the foreign players in our league. Number one, they're just not as tough as the players over here. They haven't gone through what our players do. They're given a lot of things and they play on national teams. Number two, they're not good defensively because it isn't asked of them. They don't have to play much man-to-man, and when they do it isn't against the caliber of player we have in this country.

Drazen is a tremendous offensive talent, but, and time will tell, I don't think he's ever going to be a superstar in this league. I don't see anyone yet who is going to be a superstar. I haven't seen Toni Kukoc play that much, but the longer he waits before he comes over here, the harder it's going to be for him. I think they need to come over here and play college ball to learn what our game is all about.

I definitely think some players over there can play in our league, but every time someone comes in and tells me that this guy is going to come in over here and be a superstar, I say no. For a guy to be an effective player in our league, he has to come early. You can talk about Detlef Schrempf, who came over and went to college here.

Don't tell me about a guy who is over in Europe until he's twenty-four years old and will be a superstar here. It isn't that he wouldn't have talent. It's that the type of game he would be playing over there will hurt his adjustment to the NBA.

Our game is just so much more physical. Our teams and our players simply won't allow you to do things offensively that you get used to doing over there. You're going to have to make adjustments, and from what I've seen, the European players at that age have trouble making them.

Sometimes, too, it seems that because they were usually stars at an early age—prodigies almost—they've been given a lot. They've been allowed to do whatever they want, and they don't know how to react to adversity. In our league, you're going to have to react to adversity. In our league, people sometimes are going to pummel you. It can get very tough.

Some of the Europeans are tough, but a lot are not. I look at Kukoc and he's a tremendous talent; if he came over right away, he might have a chance to be a great player. But if he waits three or four years, I don't know. That may be too much to ask.

Kukoc handles the ball, passes it and shoots it. But he plays against NBA teams once or twice a year. He would have to do it 82 games a year here, night after night where he has to go out and guard people like Dominique Wilkins and James Worthy. That's tough.

February 6, 1991

Sacramento—We're 39–8 and have just one more game before the all-star break. It turned out to be a disaster. We couldn't make a thing and were really never in the game. We only lost 97–93, but it didn't seem as if we were ever going to win the game. We just lost it. They came out and played aggressively and beat us. It wasn't the way we wanted to go into the all-star break, but we're still in first place and 39–9.

I've been hearing people say we're hearing the Lakers' footsteps coming up behind us. They've gained four-and-a-half games on us since December, and they've got a 16-game winning streak going. But we're still three games up on them. Heck, if you had told me at the start of the season that we would be 39–9 at the all-star break, I'd have been happy to take it. I don't feel the world is coming to an end just because we lost at Sacramento.

Since our team had the best record in the Western Conference, I was given the honor of coaching the West all-star team at Charlotte. I really wanted to coach in that game. Oh, I tried to make light of it during the season. I didn't think much about it early in the year when we jumped off to the great start. But as we got into January, people started asking about it and the players started talking about it a little bit. I have to admit, about that time I started looking at the schedule and trying to assess my chances. It didn't look that promising at one point.

I wanted it for a number of reasons. It's something you remember for your whole life. I don't care what anyone says, if you're a coach and have a chance to coach in an all-star game with those types of players, it's a great thrill. The closest I ever got to that game as a player was when I went to the union meeting that weekend as my team's player rep.

It was a great reward for my family and the organization and my staff. I still don't perceive myself as an all-star coach. The team got it for me. When it was still in doubt, I was a little scared to think too much about it because I didn't want to be disappointed if it didn't happen. I talked about it with my wife but nobody else. I'm sure glad it worked out.

Our two youngest kids, David and Laura, are going with Mary Kay and me, and then the two older ones, R.J. and Kathy, will join us on Saturday. So they'll all get a chance to get in on all the festivities.

I was really happy for Mary Kay to get to go. She's been an all-star for a long time.

We went to the same high school in Los Angeles, but we didn't know each other then. I knew her brother Gary, though, and he introduced us later. When we met, she didn't know anything about basketball. I remember when we first started going out and I was at a camp and said something about Jerry West. She said, "Who is Jerry West?" She lived in Los Angeles. I think Gary was there and I heard her ask him, "Who is Jerry West?" Since that time she's come a long way basketballwise. She knows an awful lot about it now. Probably more than she would care to know.

She's been such a big help to me, not so much with basketball but with perspective on things. We've been through an awful lot together. We went through the good times in Portland and the bad. I played for three different teams in one season. I was waived and didn't have a job. We packed up the family and moved to Oregon. She's been through a lot because of my profession.

You can't treat it like your whole life or it will be your whole life and you won't have anything else.

Often she'll tell me things and I'll totally disagree with her. But she understands how I deal with people and with the media, and the things she says about these two subjects are usually correct. She frequently sees things from a different angle, and we'll get into some pretty good discussions. And usually, when I have time to think about it, she's right. At the time, very often, I don't want to hear it. But she knows me better than anyone else and I listen to what she says. It helps me a lot. If I keep anything in perspective, it's because of her.

February 10, 1991

Charlotte—It was a terrific weekend because, just by coincidence, Mike Shimensky, our trainer, had already been picked as the trainer for the West. Our coaching staff was there, we had Clyde, Duck, and Terry picked to play in the game, and Danny Ainge was in the 3-point shooting contest.

It was a great experience—a reward for how well the team played in the first half of the season. I wish Buck and Jerome could have been there, too, but we just weren't going to get that many people there.

I don't think people outside of sports understand how much the trainer does or how much time he puts in. But the players know. Trainers are always on call—not only for the players and coaches, but management, the public relations and the marketing staffs, the press. Every time someone needs something he calls the trainer. It's such a time-consuming job.

Mike is tremendous. Every morning we have practice at home, he's in the training room by eight-thirty. He's there for the players, giving them treatments and getting them ready for practice by taping them. Then he's there during practice and for more treatments after practice. Then some players usually need more treatments in the afternoon, too. A lot of days, it's an off day for everyone but Mike, who is always there for the players who need him. He doesn't have any off days.

It only makes sense that when you are paying people $2

million or $3 million a year to play, you should get the best possible people to take care of them. You can save a lot of down time for your players if the trainer does his job right. I've been really fortunate with the Blazers to have Mike, and Ron Culp before him.

Trainers also have to make all the travel arrangements, including the planes, hotels, and buses. It's a thankless job sometimes, and when I think back to trainers I had when I was playing, I still remember them fondly. Some of them are still in the league, such as Billy Jones, whom I knew in Kansas City and who is with Sacramento now.

A player has a special relationship with his trainer. When you go into the trainer's room, it's your special area. I think a trainer often knows more about what's going on with a team than anyone else in the organization. He's usually a guy you can talk to, and his room is always off-limits to everyone outside the team.

I think it has to be that way—and not just for injury purposes. You obviously don't want everyone walking in and seeing who is being treated for what. But players also need a place where they can go and get away. That puts the trainer in a unique position because he has to have the confidence of the players and the confidence of the coach, too. He has to have a personality that the players can get along with. I think if they can't get along with him, he isn't going to be there long because they need someone they can trust.

If you're frustrated, he's the one you're going to talk to. Everybody is going to need him sometime during the year. I know that since I've been the head coach, if I tell Mike I want something done, it's done immediately. It's like it's over with; I don't even worry any more about it. All good trainers are like that. They take care of details and they don't forget things. Culp, who is now with Miami, was the same way. They're always protective of their team and sometimes that gets misunderstood.

I can't imagine trying to get through a season with an incompetent trainer. It would be a disaster. It used to be, back when I played, that the trainer was just somebody who took care of the equipment and taped ankles. Now they have to be certified. They used to have to work off-season jobs. Can you believe it? Here's someone taking care of million-dollar players and he wasn't being paid like a professional.

It's the same way with the team doctor. Portland is in a unique situation here, too, because of Dr. Bob Cook. The players all get along with him so well. He's just as much a friend as he is a doctor. It's not always that way in some places. Bob seems to take a little more interest in the players. I think our players are comfortable with our entire medical situation. Bob is respected worldwide. We are very fortunate he's here in Portland.

Few organizations are like the Trail Blazers. When it comes to taking care of the players, they spare no expense, and it was that way right from the start. We have quality people in important jobs, and they're dedicated. We've had Roger Sabrowski, our equipment man, almost since day one of the franchise's existence. He runs the locker room and runs it smoothly. You never want for anything. It's people like Mike and Roger who make my job easier.

Since I've been the head coach, whatever we've asked for, the attitude is, "If it makes sense, do it." A lot of organizations aren't that way. But ours really is, and I think the players who leave Portland and go somewhere else find that out real fast.

None of our players was picked to start the all-star game; all three made it by vote of the Western Conference coaches. I'm still surprised that Terry got picked. I didn't think it would happen. We had six guards, five of them point guards, and Clyde. So that made it hard to get everyone in the game. But the guys on the team were super.

What amazed me most about the whole weekend was what a good group of guys there were on that West team. I mean, they were so down-to-earth—really good guys. I think you can see why they're great players—because of the type of people they are. They were so cooperative. Magic

Johnson's been in eleven all-star games and he was there waiting to be told what to do. It was, "What would you like us to do?" They were all so coachable.

The game was tough because I had to try to get people in. Several times we were playing three point guards at the same time, trying to get everyone enough minutes. I wanted to make sure everyone got at least one quarter on the floor, and we accomplished that. But it was hard.

And what made it even harder was that such things as illegal defense are never called in this game. We were trying to spread the court and use the quickness we had, but they packed the key area against us. We couldn't keep them off the boards because they were in the lane all the time. It's funny, none of us thought anything about the money, but we all wanted to win the game. They ought to give everyone the same amount of money and just have fun.

And what is really funny is that whenever we play San Antonio, I have to beg the refs to call a foul on David Robinson. Then the one game I get to coach him, he gets three fouls in the first five minutes of the game and I have to take him out. He had five fouls in three quarters. I couldn't believe it. That really hurt us, too. I couldn't rotate our people the way I wanted to. I don't think he ever got a feel for the game because of the foul trouble.

It was kind of an unusual game. It was a lot of fun and we had a chance to win except that Karl Malone jumped up and knocked Kevin Johnson's shot away at the buzzer. He just jumped up and grabbed it right in front of the rim. I don't know if it was really going to go in, but it was close.

It was a memorable weekend for my whole family. I know Kathy and R.J. will always remember one part of it—it took them twelve hours to get there. They had to divert through Milwaukee because of fog. They were pretty wiped out but they had a great time.

February 12, 1991

Portland—We came home after the break and played Philadelphia. After a close first half, we blew it open in the third period. The game was tough because a lot of us didn't get back from Charlotte until late Monday and we had a practice that afternoon. Then we played right away on Tuesday.

It's ironic that they tell the West Coast teams not to play after Wednesday the week prior to the all-star game. They want to make sure everybody has plenty of time to get to the all-star site. So we were off Thursday, Friday, and Saturday, and the all-star game was on Sunday.

So you have three days to get to the all-star game and to get ready for it, but you've got only one day to come all the way back across the country and play a regular-season game. It would be a lot easier for the people who have to travel across country to have an extra day after the all-star game.

It's one reason I haven't gone to the game in the past. It's just so far to go. The break is great for the players who don't have to go to the game, but it's difficult for the ones who do.

And the other thing about that all-star weekend is that if you think you'll have three or four days to spend there and enjoy it, forget it. I really can't tell you what it's like in Charlotte. We got there Thursday night, then Friday was taken up with interviews and meetings. Saturday was practice, then interviews, then signing basketballs. Then they have the legends game, slam-dunk, and three-point contests Saturday night, and then the game Sunday afternoon. You're on the go constantly.

The break had a big effect on this game. Neither team played well defensively in the first half. Everybody was scoring. I told the team at halftime, as I tell them often, that the first team that made a commitment to defense was going to win. I think that's what happened against Philadelphia. We got a 15-point run and they started taking some bad shots. We just blew the game open and it ended up 121–106. It was a good win for us because after the loss to Sacramento and the break, you wonder how the team will bounce back.

Barkley has been playing well for them. He used to give us so much trouble before we got Buck. Buck forces him outside a lot more than we were able to do before. Buck does the same thing with Karl Malone. If they're going to score against us, they're going to have to work for it. It's been amazing to me that since we got Buck, Barkley hasn't been on the offensive boards as he was against us in the past. He used to just destroy us there. The last two years he's gotten some, but nothing like in the past. We just had nobody to keep him off. Now, though, Buck does that.

Buck's the most positive person I've ever been around, and on the court he's a monster. He doesn't get a lot of statistics. He doesn't score much. But I haven't seen many players who can affect a game as he does without scoring.

He creates a tempo, an atmosphere, and a tone for our team. He's the one who does that. Sometimes I don't know how he does it because he's not quick out on the floor. He's also not a big strong guy like Karl Malone. We kid him all the time that Jerome is really our power forward and he's our small forward—because Jerome is bigger than he is. But Buck is so exceptionally strong.

He can play people like Malone or Barkley—go out there and bang with them all night—and then turn around the next night and play someone like Tom Chambers or James Worthy, quick guys who take him farther out on the floor.

I admire the way he goes about it, too. He doesn't demand anything for himself. He just expects to do his job. He always plays the same way. I've seen games where teams are kicking his tail and everything's going against him, and then somewhere along the line he takes control of it. Some guys get frustrated in our league when guys score over them. That leads them to get so fouled up they take themselves out of the game.

A guy can score 20 points on Buck in the first quarter, but he's still going to have to earn every point he gets in the next three quarters. Buck has enough experience to know what's going to happen. He just keeps playing. I've seen it happen where he's just gotten killed by somebody in the first half, then suddenly in the second half the clamps come down on the guy, and because he's had to work so hard all night, Buck has beaten on him so much, the guy just doesn't have anything left.

And then when the game is on the line, Buck is going to get the ball for you. Down the stretch defensively and on the boards, he's just a monster. And what I like the most about him is that you can kid him. He takes it well. Buck's the real heart and soul of our team.

February 15, 1991

Portland—Next we played Utah and beat them 117–105. Duck had 14 rebounds and we pounded them 53–24 on the boards. It made us 41–9 and pushed us four and a half games ahead of the Lakers.

The town is really pumped up and people are still talking about us perhaps matching the 50–10 start that the 1977–78 Blazer team racked up. Sometimes people lose perspective a little.

We went out for dinner after the game and everyone wanted to talk about the game or the team. Sometimes it can really be wearing. You'd like to be able to go out once in a while and just have a normal dinner like everyone else. But this is a unique town. And it's certainly a lot more fun to talk about the team when you're 41–9 than it is when you're 25–25. People are just excited about the team. The interest seems to be increasing each day.

But sometimes I wonder if all this isn't changing me a little bit. It's almost impossible not to change with everything that's going on.

February 17, 1991

Los Angeles—Our four-and-a-half-game lead didn't last long. We had to meet the Lakers in the Forum and it wasn't much of a game. Mark Bryant broke his right foot in the first half, we were playing without Jerome again because of his calf strain, and we got beat 106–96. We just didn't play well the whole game.

With Bryant and Kersey out and Cliff Robinson in foul trouble, we didn't have anyone to guard James Worthy in the second half. He went 10 for 13 as the Lakers shot 64 percent for the half. We didn't play well, but we were still ahead by 10 in the third quarter. Then we missed 13 straight shots. They took off on a 32–11 run and took us right out of the game. They controlled the entire game.

We're totally different types of teams, but it's amazing how evenly matched we are. We have different strengths and we just kind of go back and forth, with one team holding a decent lead and the other team always coming back. The Lakers feature a great post-up game from several players—Magic, Worthy, Perkins, Divac, and Teagle. And they have very good spot-up shooters. They're intelligent and patient. Our team is very athletic and aggressive, with good penetration and offensive rebounding. We have good shooters in Terry, Danny Ainge, and Duck. The matchup just seems to make for great basketball.

February 19, 1991

Portland—We barely beat Dallas 107–100. They gave us a lot of trouble, but Cliff had another big game against them, and Clyde made a big play at the end where he knocked the ball out of Rolando Blackman's hands and we got a dunk at the other end. They thought Clyde fouled him but we didn't think so.

Danny Ainge was chasing a loose ball in this game and ran smack over Terry, who was sitting on our bench. It almost knocked Terry out because he hit the back of his head on the table near the bench. Danny was coming at us full blast, and I don't know what Terry was thinking, but he

Driving past Tom Boerwinkle of the Bulls during my playing days in Portland.

On the sidelines with Jack Ramsay, as an assistant coach for the Blazers.

My current incarnation as head coach, on the sidelines.

Terry Porter, with the ball where
I like it: in his hands.

Clyde Drexler creating in
midair.

Cliff Robinson, who's developing into such a force for us.

Kevin Duckworth shooting his reliable jumper.

Buck Williams going strong to the basket against Chicago.

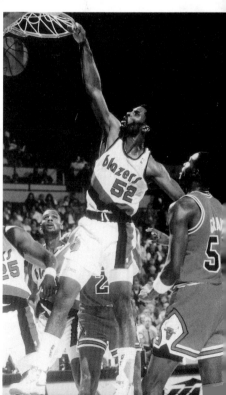

Danny Ainge, a key acquisition for our team.

Danny Young

Jerome Kersey, doing what he does so well: finishing a fast break.

I couldn't ask for better assistants than Jack Schalow (above) and John Wetzel (below).

Alaa Abdelnaby

Mark Bryant

Walter Davis

Wayne Cooper

Clyde Drexler drives toward the basket against the Lakers in the Western Conference Finals.

Jerome Kersey rejects a shot by James Worthy, also during the playoffs.

The Adelman family (left to right): my daughter, Laura, my son, R.J., my wife, Mary Kay, with my son, David, in front, me, and my daughter, Kathy.

stood up and took it full force. He was a little dingy the rest of the night. He just seemed to lose it there for a while. He said afterward that he thought Danny just wanted some extra playing time.

February 21, 1991

Denver—Same old story. We won easily and this time the Nuggets just didn't seem to play very hard. They seemed to be in a real funk.

By this time, they had modified the way they were playing. They had to; they were running out of players. Orlando Woolridge was out and so were Todd Lichti and Michael Adams. They were just trying to stay in the game at this point of the season.

We didn't dominate them, though, we just kind of stayed ahead of them. We won by 11 and I couldn't take the starters out of the game as early as I would have liked. We play at home tomorrow night against Phoenix, and they're sitting there waiting for us. But people just don't seem to understand that you have to be careful about that.

We get a 12-point lead in the third period and the fans want you to clear your bench. It used to happen all the time with Drazen. "Put in Petro," they would yell. Now I hear, "Put in Alaa." But people don't understand how quickly a game can turn. I'm always reluctant to substitute early in the fourth period. You can have a 20-point lead with eight minutes to go and people think you should just clear the bench. They want to see all those other guys play. I'd like to see those other guys play, too, and I'd like to rest my starters.

But the problem is, if you clear the bench then and put three or four subs in, and the other team hits three or four quick shots, now it's a 6- or 8-point game and you have to jerk those guys back out. Now you've lost your momentum, your starters are stiff and can't get going, and you're in a new game. And then how do those guys feel whom you put in the game? Sometimes it's not even their fault. It just happens. So I'm reluctant to do that unless I feel we're pretty much in control. Then I like to take guys out one or two at a time rather than four or five at a time.

One thing is for sure: calling the guys' names out from the grandstand isn't going to get them into the game. Fans may think it does, but it doesn't. I'll put them in the game when I feel good about it, and not until then.

I would love to give Alaa more minutes. We need him to play. We want to see what he can do. But I also need to have the other guys play, too. And this was the kind of game that was tough; we'd be up 16, then they'd cut it down to 10. It wasn't until about two minutes to go that I was certain we would win. Then I hate to throw someone in there who hasn't played all night and ask him to play forty-five seconds. Sometimes I do that if I have to, because someone is tired and needs to come out.

Because of the game tomorrow night, I did put some guys in this one very late and they acted as if it were an intrusion on them.

I understand that because I was in that situation as a player, too. I was thrown into games with thirty seconds to go, and I know how it feels when you've been sitting there all night. It's like, ''Well, what do you want me to do now?'' But the fact of the matter is, the players are getting paid a good salary, and if I put him in there for ten seconds or forty minutes, he's supposed to play. And I told some of them after the game that if they didn't, then they were never going to get into a game.

It's a two-way street. If they aren't going to go out there and play when I ask them to, then in the games that are 20- and 30-point games, when they have a chance to play seven or eight minutes, forget it. Especially on a team such as ours. If I have to take Buck Williams or Clyde Drexler out because I don't want to see them get hurt and we have an important game the next night, I don't want to have to explain it or put up with anyone's annoyance. I don't want to see it.

I think I got my point across. Alaa was one of the guys I was talking to after this game, and it was the first time all season he did that. He was just mad and acted as if he didn't want to be there. An attitude like that is the quickest way to get a bad reputation around the league.

You go into the game when the coach tells you, and you bust your rear end and then no one questions you. That way you don't hurt yourself in anyone's eyes—let alone your own coach's. I wanted to make that clear to Alaa especially, though I never worried about him. He handled everything well all year.

I still remember what happened in San Diego when Elvin Hayes and I were rookies playing for Jack McMahon. We had a great first year with six rookies, and we still got into the playoffs and shocked everyone by taking Atlanta to six games before losing. We were a very good team.

Everyone thought the next year we were going to be one of the up-and-coming teams, but it all fell apart.

Elvin at the time was a lot like Sidney Wicks would be later in Portland. I mean he did everything. He scored, rebounded, passed, blocked shots. He was the guy. So all the pressure was on him. If things were going to go good, Elvin was the reason. But Elvin was also very young and not as mature as he would later become. And he had the owner's ear. At times Jack would try to get us to do things and Elvin would have some problems and just leave practice. And Jack couldn't fine him because he would go to the owner and the owner would pat him on the back and say everything was going to be okay.

I remember, too, when Jack McCloskey came to Portland, he was going to take care of all the problems we had. You know, he was an ex-Marine, straight out of college coaching, and he knew nothing about our league at the time. Now you look at Jack McCloskey and what he has done—he built the Detroit Pistons into a championship team. No one knows the league better now than Jack.

But at that time he was going to put his foot down. He was going to discipline our team. But it didn't work out.

The only thing Jack could have done, I guess, was beat the hell out of Sidney. But Sidney wasn't going to back down. I think Jack learned so much through his experience in Portland and then being an assistant to Jerry West at Los Angeles.

But I remember one time at the Jewish Community Center in Portland at one of our practices when Jack was getting on Sidney and Sidney just rebelled. They had a big shouting match right there on the floor with a lot of people around. What can you do? There's nothing you can do. You can't win. Jack couldn't win. Sidney couldn't win.

You don't want to get in a confrontation with your players out in front of everyone. If they happen, you want those things to happen in private.

But I never liked to be called out in public, either. I don't believe that's the way to do things. Sometimes you have to get on players. You have to talk to them. But I firmly believe in doing it in general terms only in front of the group. Then if I want to talk to a player individually, I call him in and talk it through.

That may be the right or wrong way to do it—a lot of coaches are successful jumping all over their guys in front of everyone and their guys respond. But it's just not the way I do it. I've had coaches do that to me and I hated it. I felt at the time, you're jumping all over me, but what about some of these other guys? Don't just pick on me. It's not a good way for a player to think. I think coaches who do that have two or three guys that they pick on all the time, and they'll let it go with somebody else.

I wasn't going to do that. If I couldn't get on every guy the same way, I wasn't going to get on anyone. Some guys do respond to it, but if you call a guy down, you better be ready for his reaction. You better understand what may happen.

After Jack McMahon got fired in San Diego, they brought in Alex Hannum. There were stories that Alex had backed Wilt Chamberlain down. I know I saw him back Elvin down one day in practice. I think Elvin was afraid that Alex was going to kill him. Alex had that bald head and was about six foot eight and was big and strong. When he got mad, his forehead turned red and you knew you were in trouble.

He got mad in practice one time when we were running lines and Alex really wanted us to go hard. We were running a three-man weave and Elvin had a way of just working himself into it and going through the motions. Alex told him to pick it up, but Elvin just stayed in the same trot. They had a few exchanges and Elvin still stayed in the same trot.

The next thing we knew Alex kicked everyone out of practice except Elvin. He told everyone to get off the floor and go into the locker room. We had heard stories about Alex going toe-to-toe with Wilt, so we all went around the corner and waited, listening and peeking to see what was going to happen.

Sure enough, Alex backed Elvin right up against the wall and basically told him, if you aren't going to do it my way, you and I are going to go at it right here and whoever walks out . . . I think Elvin had never run into anybody like that before. Elvin would have had to kill him to win his point. Finally Alex called us back in and told us we were going to run the three-man weave again and we were going to *run*. We were all wondering what would happen.

We started the three-man weave again and Elvin took off like a bat out of hell. I think he thought Alex was a nut. But that's how Alex was. You do it my way or we're going to have it out. I couldn't believe it. I wouldn't have fooled with him, either. He got his point across and he got his way.

But I don't think I could ever pull that on anybody. Not unless I handpicked the guy, anyway. That just isn't my style. I'm not going to beat anybody up. And one thing holds true in this league: you've got to be yourself. If you don't, the players are going to see through you right away. If you're going to succeed, you have to understand how you're going to handle these guys because handling guys is the biggest part of the job.

I don't believe in calling people out. I try not to embarrass people on the sideline. But I don't want them to embarrass me with their actions, either. I've told them that a number of times and I think they understand that.

February 22, 1991

Portland—While we were beating the Nuggets last night, Phoenix was sitting in their hotel rooms in Portland waiting to play us tonight. And they didn't even have to have cable television in their rooms to watch us play because we telecast the game back home on a local station. It always seems to work out that way whenever anyone is sitting in Portland waiting for us. It's as if we always reserve the right to give them that extra edge.

Actually, though, it turned out to be a great game for us. We won 127–106, and two incredible statistics came out of the game: we had only three turnovers for the entire game— an NBA record—and Kevin Johnson had only one assist for them. That's almost impossible, because he has the ball in his hands all the time.

I thought this would be a much closer game because Phoenix needed to win, because they were closing in on the Lakers and us and they had been playing well. But we just played so well. We were so good defensively and we ran the ball well. They couldn't stay with us. It was a terrific win against a team that was coming at us, and we had played the night before at Denver. We're 4½ games ahead of the Lakers, and 6½ up on the Suns.

February 24, 1991

Portland—This is a great example of how you just never know in our league. I don't care what anybody says, you just don't know when you're going to get on a roll and you don't know when you're going to have a tough time. We beat Denver at Denver, then came home and played a terrific game against Phoenix. And then we played a real downer of a game.

I don't see how anyone could have predicted that. The confidence factor in this league is so fragile. We were confident, we were 44–10, we were playing at home and coming off a terrific game. But we had San Antonio coming to town, and the results were disappointing.

I was surprised we played so poorly. After beating Phoenix and scoring almost 130 points, we turned right around and scored 88 at home against San Antonio and lost 95–88. We were lackluster the whole game. The first time we played San Antonio was the game where we had that terrific first quarter, but tonight it was almost as if we thought we were going to win so we could just go out and play this time. We were awful. And actually, San Antonio had been really struggling lately and we had been playing well.

But we used really poor judgment in this game. We made only 4 of 21 3-point field goals. In the fourth quarter, we took some 3s that we didn't really have to take. Jerome got kicked out of this game for kicking the ball, which really hurt us.

I would never have predicted this to happen. I talked to David Robinson at their shooting practice the morning before the game, and he and Willie Anderson were talking about how they were just struggling and they didn't know what was going on. They seemed to be really down. I told Willie, "You guys will snap out of that. It's just a matter of time. You've had all those injuries. You just have to keep your head up." But I didn't expect him to do it so quickly; he got 25 against us that night.

They really packed the paint against us, the first time they've been effective doing that. We didn't move their people around very well, and Robinson just never left the lane the whole game. And we didn't shoot well enough to make up for it.

That's how quickly fortunes can change in this league. And that's why I think you've got to have the ability to respond and not get down—even when everybody around you is down. You have to keep pushing because then you'll break through and be okay.

February 26, 1991

San Antonio—That's right, we had to play San Antonio again at their place in our next game. We went down there and played a first half that was worse than how we had played in the game at our place.

I couldn't believe how bad we were. It was as if we had never played the game together before in our lives. We were stumbling around, missing lay-ups and open shots. The incredible thing is that we weren't down by 25 points at halftime, as bad as we played. We scored only 27 points in the first half, but we were lucky because they had only 44.

I kind of went off at halftime. We had talked a lot about the way San Antonio had defended us in the game at Portland, and we looked at a lot of tape. I was worried that they were doing something we hadn't seen before or something was going on we didn't see. Something, that is, besides Robinson standing around in that zone of his, which he does a lot.

We have all these rules about illegal defense, but what blows me away is, if I'm the official out there on the floor and here's a seven-foot-one guy on the floor standing right in the middle of the lane—I think all I'd have to do is turn my head and see that guy and wonder where his man is. But it's as if they don't see that. It seems so easy. All they have to do is make one or two calls, and whatever the defense is doing is going to change. By not calling it, though, you encourage it to continue.

And often, they'll tell the offensive team to prove the defense is illegal. Here we are with a 24-second clock and it's usually down to about eighteen seconds by the time you get the ball up the court, and you have to prove they're illegal and still get a good shot opportunity. That makes no sense to me, but that's what they tell us—show us it's illegal. If it's illegal, just nail them and they won't do it anymore and then you don't have to worry about it anymore.

We thought he was zoning all night. We looked at the tape and they weren't doing anything defensively except dragging through the lane, watching the ball, when we were running our motion offense. But we weren't moving, we were walking away or standing and watching the guy with the ball. So their defenders were in great position to stop us whenever we tried to get to the basket. David Robinson never had to move the whole night.

So, anyway, I was a little upset at halftime. I just said, this is the team that beat the hell out of us in San Antonio in the playoffs last year, and they had just beaten us at our place. We were either going to have to make a commitment to change in the second half, or they're going to have our number. We have to show what kind of team we are in the second half of this game, and we have to be more aggressive.

I doubt it was the speech that did it, but we were down 19 in the third quarter, and suddenly it was as if our guys just opened up. We started playing and started competing. We got aggressive again. We started moving people around offensively. Suddenly that miraculous defense they played for six quarters wasn't there and we were getting shots at the basket. We were getting to the free-throw line. Everything started going our way. We got all the way back in the second half, and Buck went to the free-throw line with no time left on the clock and the score tied.

The free throw went in and out on him. And then we lost 102–101 in overtime. We didn't execute the play we wanted for the last shot of overtime, and Buck ended up with the ball for a hurried shot.

I was disappointed in the first half, but I felt good about the second half. I need to feel good because we're on an awfully tough trip. We've lost two straight and have to go play Atlanta, a hot team, and Philadelphia, who are always hard to beat at their place. We were on top of the world two games ago—and now we're trying to figure out what's wrong. It doesn't make any sense.

February 28, 1991

Atlanta—We had a nice lead at the start of the fourth quarter against the Hawks, but we lost 117–109. It was the first time all season we had a lead at the end of the third quarter and lost. I substituted at the start of the fourth—the same guys I always use at the start of the final quarter—but we seemed to lose all offensive sync at the start of the period. They got some easy baskets because of the way we were playing offensively, and the momentum changed. Atlanta is the type of team, too, that if you let them get the momentum, they can be like us—they can catch a spurt and run over anybody. If you defend them and you're smart offensively, which we were for three quarters, they get frustrated and they'll take tougher shots and they aren't as confident. But we didn't do that at the start of the fourth quarter and they turned the whole game around on us.

Three straight losses. And we have to start next month with games at Philadelphia and Boston. The lead is down to a game and a half. Things are probably going to get worse before they get better.

March

March 1, 1991

Philadelphia—A three-game losing streak and a date at the Spectrum against the 76ers is not an inviting prospect. They're tough at home and Barkley is hard to handle there.

I think Barkley is a product of our league in a lot of ways. He's a tremendous player. He just amazes me with the things he does. He isn't tall but he's just so powerful. He does incredible things offensively. He's a great passer and an improved outside shooter.

On the other hand, he can be very critical of his teammates and other people. He says what he feels because he's always been encouraged to do so. The league wants our games to be a show. They hype people and he's one of the people they hype as a kind of good bad guy. A lot of times I think he's just going along with it. He likes being a showman, and before he knows it, because he speaks his mind, he'll react to a situation and say something or do something that he shouldn't.

But I think you can't blame him sometimes. He's just being Charles Barkley. I know one thing, he plays the game hard and he's about as competitive as you can get. And there's a lightheartedness about him that lets him joke with the other team or laugh with the fans.

We lost to the Sixers 121–111 but we really didn't play too badly. It was one of those typical road games where you compete but you just can't ever get over the hump. I think we were a little bit tired and down because we had lost three in a row. Every time we started to make a little run at them, they'd make a big shot or get a steal—or we would turn it over to them. We just never got back into it once we got behind.

I'm really beginning to get frustrated because we aren't getting to the free-throw line. I don't understand it. I didn't feel we'd changed our game that much, but suddenly the other team is getting to the line twice as much as we are.

We're taking it to the basket just as much as ever and we aren't getting any calls. I'm sure there are times when everything is going good for me and some other coach is yelling about the same thing. This is what always happens when you are not playing well. Tonight we had 10 more field goals than them and we lost the game by 10 points. At Atlanta, we shot 17 free throws and they shot 40. In the game at Philly, we were around the basket all night and just didn't get any calls.

Kevin Duckworth seldom gets a call. I defy anybody in the league office or any official in this league to tell me—if they looked at the tape objectively—that he doesn't get fouled when he shoots the ball about half the time. Duck doesn't jump high on his shots, and he's so big and so strong that if someone pushes him or nudges him on his body, it doesn't torque like David Robinson's or Patrick Ewing's does. You can't move him like you can other people, but he's getting hit continuously on the body and he never—never—gets that call.

If Duck goes to the line, it's because he's pump-faked somebody in the air and they came down on his shoulder. I never see him get a call for anybody pushing him on his body.

I have been told that Duckworth and a couple of other guys are really good at doing one thing: when a guy goes up for a shot, they put their hands in the air straight up, but then they move in underneath the guy and body him. That's a foul. I'll buy that. He does that some. He moves in sometimes. But can you tell me why he doesn't get that same call when someone does that to him?

The difference is he doesn't go anywhere. But they're still affecting his shot. They bump him. That's a foul.

The greatest comment about this came from an official whom I won't name, who worked a game of ours last season. Duck got the ball and spun through the middle to shoot a hook shot, and Pervis Ellison had not one but two hands on Duck's waist. I'm standing right there and the official is to my left, and you can see Ellison's arms extended, pushing Duck. Kevin rolls across the lane, gets pushed, and there's no whistle.

He misses, we get the offensive rebound and get fouled, and I'm going nuts. I said, "You can't be serious. Are you kidding me?" And the comment to me from the official was, "You mean a hundred-and-eighty-pound guy is going to bother his shot?"

And that's the story. They don't think he gets hit very hard and he's so big and strong that they think it shouldn't bother him. But I'm hoping that the longer he plays and the more we talk about it, maybe it will get looked at a little closer.

When you're losing, these kinds of things really get to you. They eventually even out through the season, but it's frustrating, especially on the road.

At home, I try to stay on an even keel as much as possible, especially when I'm in the office. I can't imagine a front-office staff any more supportive than Portland's. Our office has expanded during my eight years on the coaching staff. Unfortunately, during the season, it is hard to see the people in our office. We're on the road so much and I try to stay at home as much as I can when we are not traveling. As a result, I don't see a lot of the people who make things run smoothly. Occasionally, I will go into the office in the morning to get my mail, answer phone calls, or go to a meeting. I have my video equipment at home and I watch tapes there. Every coach is different. Mike Schuler liked office hours. He went in most days to get his mail and to make phone calls. Jack Ramsay would go in but not as often as Mike. Everyone has his own way of doing things.

Fortunately, in the last two years, we have won most of our games. As a result, there has been mostly excitement around our office. I remember not too long ago it wasn't always this way.

When a team is struggling it can change the whole atmosphere. Nobody really knows what to say to a player or coach when things are not going well. When you are coaching a team that is struggling, it's hard to break out of a somber mood. You don't even realize that you are making those around you "walk on eggs." If things are bothering me or we are losing, I find I can get myself out of that mood a lot easier in my home than at the office—where you are reminded of it all the time. If you are in the office, basketball is all you think about. Therapeutically, for me, it's better not to go in, and probably better for those in the office, too.

I think I've gotten worse about all that this season because of the pressure involved and the outside distractions. Last year I would go to the office and try not to be a downer if things weren't going good.

Sometimes I don't even realize what I'm doing and I'm thinking about something and someone will walk past me and think, jeez, he didn't even say hello. I don't want to hurt anyone's feelings, but it happens. It's easier for me just not to be there.

I remember during Jack's last days as our coach, I saw some things happen with him. When Jack started to lose, and we lost ten or twelve games in a row at one stretch, people around the office started to take shots at him. It was really apparent. Jack would come down the hallway and people would actually turn around and walk the other way so they wouldn't have to run into him.

I remember one instance in particular where a guy who worked in our front office said on the elevator that they should fire Jack. Right there in an elevator full of a bunch of people he didn't know! It was incredible. If a coach had said that about him, the coach would have been called on the carpet. If I comment on someone else in the organization, they call me in and tell me I can't do that.

The biggest problem in professional sports—for athletes and coaches—is that only one thing matters: I could be the greatest person ever to walk into this office, the nicest guy in the whole wide world, do everything you want me to do, and if I lose games, I'm out. It all comes down to wins and losses.

That's the bottom line. I mean it's not totally true. But it's close. As a head coach you need the support of management. You need someone to bounce ideas off of and get different points of view from about the team. You need someone besides your assistant coaches. But it's hard to get a feel for what's right and what's wrong with the team unless you're close to it.

To know the situation you have to be around the team every day like the coach is. You have to know the problems he has and what he's trying to do about them. And you have to give the guy some input. If you have an idea or a suggestion that may help, offer it. The coach can then either accept that or reject it.

I'm lucky now because I have Geoff Petrie in that role and he's been terrific. He was a roommate of mine as a player, and now he's running the basketball side of our operation. He's in every meeting and knows exactly what's going on with our team.

Frequently, when the wheels start falling off in the NBA, the coach is usually just out there by himself. It can happen to anybody. Jack Ramsay was here ten years and won a championship. If it can happen to Jack, it can happen to anybody.

March 3, 1991

Boston—We had a day off before facing the Celtics, and I
know everybody's really down. There's a lot of "What's
wrong with us?" going on. I've got to try to change the
atmosphere around the team. We've got a whole week off
after this game, and I know how long that's going to seem
if we go into it having lost five straight.

We didn't practice the day before the game because we
never do after back-to-back games. The last thing I want to
do is alter that routine. I want to relax everybody as much
as possible. We have to take a low-key approach to this
game. I want to try to take the pressure off everyone; this
is no time to panic.

I did feel we'd come out and play well because we always
seem to play well at Boston. I wanted us to come out and
just play and forget about everything that's been happening
to us. We weren't playing as poorly as everyone said we
were.

Then we went out and the first half of the the game was
almost identical to what had happened in the three previous
games. We didn't shoot a free throw in the whole first half—
which, in itself, is amazing. It wasn't as if we were settling
for jump shots. We were taking the ball to the basket. We
were playing hard and aggressively.

I told the team at halftime to just keep playing the way
they were playing. I couldn't see anything we were doing
wrong, except on the scoreboard, where we were trailing
56–51. As far as I could see, we were back to where we
were before, playing with a lot of energy. We kept doing it
in the second half, and suddenly we started getting to the
foul line. We got there twenty-six times in the second half
and won the game 116–107. We flat-out beat them and
played a solid game all the way through. It made the flight
home a lot easier.

March 10, 1991

Portland—After the game at Boston we didn't play again until we met the Celtics at Portland a week later. Originally, the schedule had called for us to come west from Boston and play at Sacramento Tuesday night, but we asked the league to change it. We said, wait a minute—we play at San Antonio, Atlanta, Philadelphia, and Boston, and then you're going to send us back to Sacramento? That's a five-game trip and we're making a complete circle before we get home.

Sacramento is only an hour and a half away, we said. Can we find another day to play them? The league went along and it was switched to another date, and that's how we ended up with a whole week off in the middle of the season. It worked out great for me because my oldest son, R.J., was playing in the boys' state basketball tournament in Memorial Coliseum and I got a chance to see him play four games, after missing practically every game during his regular season. My oldest daughter, Kathy, had played in the state tournament three different seasons, and all I got to see was one game and one quarter of another.

As a kid, I was lucky. My family has always been into basketball and was very supportive.

My parents, L.J. and Gladys Adelman, moved out to California from North Dakota to find a new life. They had both been teachers and farmers in North Dakota, but when he got to California, my father went to work for the U.S. Borax Corp. He worked his way up to office manager and eventually managed an office building in Los Angeles for thirty-something years.

My mother and father have a tremendous work ethic. They did everything for their six children. We weren't rich but never really wanted for anything because of their support and unselfishness. I believe their perseverance and strong character was instilled in our whole family.

I have had great support not only from my parents but from my sisters and brothers, JoAnne, Patty, Clete, Monica, and Frank. The closeness of our family is a direct reflection of the values my parents gave us. Whenever we are playing on the road close to where one of them lives, they go out of their way to see us play. If things are tough, I will always get a phone call to see how I am holding up.

One of the best things about this year is that Mom and Dad moved to Oregon recently, and they have the chance to see the Blazers play a lot. There are no more loyal fans than L.J. and Gladys Adelman.

We moved to Compton when I was four or five, and one of the first things my dad did was to put a hoop up on the garage. It was a wrought-iron hoop, bolted to the roof of the garage with a backboard that was square, made from a hardwood floor. It was regulation-sized and everything.

We moved later and put another hoop on our new garage. I drove by that first place in Compton about five or six years ago and I didn't recognize much about that house; when you're young everything seems bigger than it actually is. The house looks so small now. But that backboard was still on the garage roof. The rim was gone, but you couldn't take that backboard down without taking the whole garage roof down.

Our week off between Celtics games didn't do us much good. I gave the team a couple of days off, and when we practiced we worked mostly on our offense, trying to be more consistent. But Boston came into our building and beat us 111–109 in overtime. At the end of regulation we got a wide-open shot for Terry Porter—dead-open from sixteen feet, all by himself, but it hit the back rim and went out. Then we lost in overtime. It was our reliable 2-out play and it got us the shot we wanted; we just missed it.

We made some mistakes in this game, though. We didn't execute well. You have to give Boston credit. They played a solid game. But we had now lost five out of six.

There's been much talk in the Portland media about why we were struggling. Many people thought we were unbeatable because of the preseason buildup and quick start. Our win at Boston seemed to defuse a lot of the negative feeling. That game was televised and many people immediately felt we were back on the right track. Now there'll be all those questions again.

March 11, 1991

Portland—We beat Cleveland 104–96 but didn't play too well. It was plain we were out of our rhythm.

What's so strange about this whole period is that we've had games like the win over Boston in it. It's not as if we're totally out of sync for two weeks. We played pretty well at Philadelphia and very well for the second half at San Antonio. We played well at Boston.

But during this slide every team we've played was a very good team. Against lesser teams, we would have won a lot of those games even though we weren't playing well. It's been a difficult time in our schedule, though, and we just haven't gotten over the hump. We just don't seem to have the energy we had earlier in the season.

We all have some ideas about what's going on and we talked among ourselves, but we hadn't gotten together yet. I'm not much for calling team meetings. You don't want to call many or they lose their effect. But we've been so up and down.

March 13, 1991

Phoenix—We got killed by the Suns. Phoenix just ran right over the top of us. Dan Majerle hurt us and Andrew Lang and Mark West destroyed us on the offensive boards. We couldn't box them out. If they missed a shot, they got it back and scored. That's usually what we do to them.

They beat us in every part of the game, and the final score (116–108) is deceiving. It wasn't an 8-point game.

Chicago passed us after this game in the race for the best

record in the league. Everybody is creeping up on us. We're only a game and a half ahead of L.A., and Phoenix reacted as if they had won a playoff game. They were really pumped up.

Actually, Phoenix got a little too excited. You get that excited over a regular-season game and you're liable to go out pretty flat the next game.

We canceled tomorrow's practice and scheduled a meeting at our hotel before flying *Blazer I* to Salt Lake City and a game in two days against the Jazz.

March 14, 1991

Phoenix—We're so frustrated that a practice wasn't going to do us a lot of good, anyway. We haven't had a lot of meetings, and so I thought maybe it was a good time to get together. I didn't expect any major pronouncements; I just wanted everyone to have a chance to speak.

No one was going to start pointing fingers at anybody because our guys aren't like that and our problems have been more general. But I think we all need to focus on what we had to do. We planned on the coaches saying what we had to say and then leaving, letting the players talk it out among themselves. But Jerome thought we should stay. He said if they had something to say, we should hear it. So I said okay, and the coaches stayed.

It wasn't anything startling. A lot of the guys talked. Just about everyone said something. It came down, though, to the same thing over and over again: we have to start playing harder. It isn't that they don't want to play, they just aren't playing with the same fire and aggressiveness that they have to have to be really good. We're playing in stretches, but not with the fire we have when we're really active.

We had been a little flat. The players felt the only way they were going to get back to where we were was to start defending people again. If we start defending and rebounding better, the offense will take care of itself. We have to play with emotion, and the energy it gives us. We can't just fall back and rely on shooting the ball.

There was some discussion that when we're on offense and we call a play, we should try to execute the play and not take the first thing someone gives us. We should try to make them defend us a little bit.

Duck was pretty funny, because when he finally got a chance to talk, he said that everyone was basically saying the same damn thing over and over and he said, "Why don't we just go out and do it? That's our problem. We're talking about it but we're not going out on the court and doing anything about it."

I think everyone agreed with that.

The other thing that came up was that we'd always been a positive team to each other and that some of the guys on the bench weren't into the game the way they were before. There wasn't any encouragement. Guys were just letting guys play. When someone made a good play, there was no response to it. But that's getting back, again, to having the fire, having the excitement, the enthusiasm, in what you are doing.

We were afraid this was what was going to happen to us at the start of the year because we had gotten to the Finals the year before. We had had such a good year it would have been easy to expect everything to come easy for us. But we didn't do that at the start of the year. We started the season on a positive note, but we seem to have gotten complacent. Everything had been easy and we just expected to win. But we hadn't been doing what we needed to do to win.

You want to have that confidence, but you also need to realize you've got to keep working, keep some of the hunger that got you there in the first place. Maybe we needed to hit some adversity to realize that. Maybe it was the best thing that happened to us, because it opened our eyes a little bit. After our start, everybody was pointing toward us. Look at Phoenix: they beat us and it was as if it were a championship game for them. It was so important for them. It's almost like what happens to teams when they win the title. But we haven't won anything yet. We've got to remember that and get back the hunger.

Our guys realized that and talked it through. When you have a meeting like this, you're just trying to do anything that will light the spark or get it all to go the other way. It's nothing earth-shattering, but I think it can help.

March 15, 1991

Salt Lake City—The meeting obviously did help. And that was the last thing I said to them at the meeting—there's no better place to turn it around than the place where everybody expected us to lose.

I remember clearly while I was driving somewhere and someone asked Steve Jones, "Will the Blazers ever win at Utah?" He said something like, "When it snows in hell." He said we have no chance to win in Utah, which I couldn't quite believe. I mean, we haven't played well there, but there's always a chance, although I did understand why Steve said it.

So we went in and beat them 106–96. We played a solid game and controlled the tempo. We defended them well, and for the first time in my memory, we played well offensively in the Salt Palace. We moved their people and were in control of the game. Once we got ahead by about 10 in the fourth quarter, it was over.

It looks good because we had that team meeting and then suddenly, we went out and beat Utah at Utah. Everything looks good. I think we are finally over the hump, because we played so well. Clyde has struggled at Utah in the past, but he was unbelievable in this game. He was all over the court. We made a statement in this game. We wanted to get back to playing the way we had played earlier—and we did.

March 17, 1991

Portland—We aren't over the hump at all.

We came home and lost 107–97 to the Clippers, and I hope it will be the real wake-up call for us this time. We had been losing to some good teams on the road, but that's nothing like losing to the Clippers at home. Our players are embarrassed and they should be.

Maybe the Utah game hurt us because it made things look too easy. I think in a way, coming on the heels of that meeting, it led us to believe that we could just turn the switch on and play well whenever we felt like it.

This was just an awful game. But maybe it's the jolt we need to kick us into gear. They hadn't won at Portland in years, and we just played so poorly that they actually controlled the fourth quarter on us. They did all the things they had to do to win the game.

March 19, 1991

Oakland—We got blitzed in our next game, too, a 136–126 loss at Golden State. But this was different. The Warriors came out on fire and we couldn't do anything with them in the first half. Mitch Richmond came out and made every shot he took. He was unbelievable. They beat us up and down the court, and even when we did get back, they pulled up and made jump shots. We were behind 64–35 in the second quarter and 82–58 at the half. I was awestruck at halftime. There was nothing I could say.

So I changed my approach and said, hey, they were near perfect in the first half and all we can do is just try to come back. I told them to just forget the first half and forget the Clipper game and use the second half to build for the rest of the season. We did that. We came back from being about 30 points behind and almost won and I was really pleased.

But with that loss, we fell out of first place in the division. And now we're going to see what we're made of.

March 20, 1991

Los Angeles—Our rematch with the Clippers was not a pretty game. We didn't play well, but I think we played hard. The Lakers lost to Seattle and we won 100–96, so we moved back into first place by a half game. We had been out of the top spot for just twenty-four hours.

We mostly felt relief after the win. We just wanted to get back to winning on the road again.

Of course, the other thing that happened was that Jerome started playing again. He had missed so much practice time and was really out of sync. But he's getting his game together again, and when he's playing well, we're a different team.

He's changed his pregame routine. You can't talk to him before the game anymore. He's almost like a prizefighter. He won't talk. He'll listen at the meeting, and when the meeting is over, most of the guys will go to the bathroom or they'll talk or they'll walk around. He just sits over there in the corner with a towel around his neck and partly over his head. He just sits there.

I keep thinking he's going to go out and punch somebody. He's just so in tune and so focused. He has a great way of getting himself ready. But it's kind of new, and I asked him if he was getting ready to fight Mike Tyson or something.

March 24, 1991

Portland—We went home and beat Charlotte 117–102. A win's a win, but I can't enjoy it. We're heading into the toughest part of our schedule. I always play this game where I look at everyone's schedule and try to figure where we'll end up. We're looking at back-to-back games against Seattle—with the Sonics now playing their best basketball of the season—then a road game against the Lakers, and after a home game against Minnesota, a six-game road trip that includes a three-game trip to Texas, followed by the Lakers at home. Ouch. If we don't get back to the way we were playing earlier, we'll be in third place in a week or two.

And I still can't get rid of this cold. In fact, I'm putting on weight for the first time in my life, and I find myself just staying in my room while we're on the road. I'm too tired to do much of anything. I hate the road. Whose idea was it to play so many games, anyway?

March 26, 1991

Portland—We beat the Sonics by 13. We were all over them for two and a half quarters. They couldn't do anything. Then we let them back in the game and they cut our lead to 3 with two minutes to play. Will we ever stop letting teams come back? But Terry and Clyde made some big plays down the stretch, and the final score was a little wider than it should have been. It wasn't that easy.

We were 19 points ahead going into the final period and we just stopped moving. Ricky Pierce got it going and they made a big run at us. But we won, and now we go up to play Seattle again the next game at Tacoma.

March 27, 1991

Tacoma—I took Mary Kay to the game with me and we were sitting upstairs prior to the game watching the fans come in. I told her it seemed like a home game because of all the people carrying signs for our team. They were yelling and screaming when our players came out of the locker room to shoot.

I didn't know it at the time, but Seattle didn't give that

game to its season ticket holders; they just sold tickets to anyone who wanted them. Many people in Portland can't buy tickets to home games because we're always sold out, and they figured out that tickets to this game were available. So they not only bought them, they were pumped up because for a lot of them, this was the only game they'd get to see all season.

It was weird. It made for a strange atmosphere all night—like a college game with fans roaring for every basket by either team. They would score and we would score, and half the arena would erupt on every play.

We couldn't make a shot in the second quarter and they were playing well. We were down 24 at the start of the third quarter. When you get down like that, there's nothing you can do but just try. You've certainly got to try to defend them—somehow, some way. We needed to do that and to rebound.

We told them at halftime we just wanted to cut it down and get in a position in the fourth quarter to have a chance to win. You say that as a coach sometimes at halftime, but you don't really know if it's possible. It's hard to believe sometimes it can happen. You're just hoping you can somehow turn it around.

But Duck started running the floor well and getting to spots. We made some intelligent passes and gave him room to operate. Then we began moving the ball so well they couldn't lock their defense in. The end of the game was incredible. We were 3 down with three minutes to go, and they barely scored the rest of the game.

By this time the place was going crazy. It was just crazy. We ended up winning 112–107, and it was the best comeback we'd had all season. It's hard to beat anybody back-to-back in this league, and that made it even more satisfying. And it set the tone for us, because we have to go to L.A. next. But we feel as if we're back in control of our own destiny.

March 29, 1991

Los Angeles—Our game against the Lakers shapes up as probably one of our biggest all season because we've lost two of three to them and we need to win this one to have any chance of capturing the season series. So we went out and promptly fell 17 points behind at halftime. I wasn't real happy, and in fact, I just about went nuts at halftime.

We've come so far and here's a team that we've always challenged in the past and we've always come up short against them—probably because they've always had a better team than us. We've been talking all year about winning the divison from them, we had a day's rest after two great wins over Seattle, and we came out in the first half and just didn't compete.

They were dominating the game. They were the aggressors. Worthy was killing us and we weren't rotating defensively. We weren't playing well offensively. I knew the players were also very upset at halftime. It's one thing to go into a game like this and lose; it's another to be 17 down at halftime. We're a good team, so there's just no reason to be down like that at halftime. It was ridiculous.

I was very frustrated that we couldn't come out and play a better half than that, and when I got in there with the players, I could hear they were upset, too. I kicked one of those metal rollaway training tables with all the tape and everything on it. I didn't really mean to kick it that hard, but it was pretty light. I walked in and started to talk, and this thing was sitting right there in front of me and I just gave it a kick—and everything on it just went flying. I think it got everyone's attention.

Then I ripped the way we approached the game. I told them I just didn't understand; after everything we had gone through and all the things we'd done, then we came out in a game like this and played like that? I told them I didn't even think we were competing. We weren't even trying to take it to them. We were letting them do whatever they wanted. We weren't challenging them.

I told them if we were going to lose, we were going to do it with a performance such as we had the second half against Seattle. We weren't going to go down playing the way we did in the first half.

We went out in the third quarter and fell 21 back. And then I can't even tell you what happened or why, but we caught them before the end of the third period. It was one of the few times I can remember a Laker team becoming totally disjointed against us. We were all over them.

We switched Buck over to guard Worthy. He had been shooting over the top of Jerome. We told Buck to push him out, and it gave Jerome a chance to be more active on the rotations. We took them out of the game for the rest of the quarter in one of the best defensive performances we've ever seen. We were getting our hands on balls, deflecting passes, taking away the dribble. Every time they turned it over or missed, we were getting dunks at the other end. We outscored them 27–4 in the last eight minutes of the third quarter.

In the fourth quarter it was anybody's game, and to their credit they came out and seemed to be in control. They had us down by 8 with four minutes to go, but we scored 9 straight points. It was unbelievable. We got it into overtime and then Duck fouled out and Cliff fouled out. Terry blocked a lay-up by Magic—one of only 11 blocks for him all season—and we ran about three balls down in the open court. We won 109–105 and it was an amazing win, coming right after that comeback against Seattle.

Those two comebacks had us flying high again.

March 30, 1991

Portland—What really impressed me was that we had to come back home the next night and play Minnesota and we just crushed them. In the past, we've struggled with those games. But we beat them by 30. We took command and you could see fire in our eyes. We were really back on track.

We were confident again. We're up by three games in the division again and we're just a game behind Chicago for the best record overall. All of the things that looked as if they had slipped away were suddenly back in focus.

We open the final month of the season with a six-game road trip. But we're feeling pretty good about ourselves again.

April

April 2, 1991

Minneapolis—It's going to be the longest road trip of the year. I don't ever remember a Portland team going on a six-game trip in April; usually you're in your own conference this time of the year. We have to go east, then to Florida and to Texas, so it's going to be a difficult and long journey.

I look at the first four games as the key ones. They're games where you look at it and everybody says, well, we should win those—Minnesota, Washington, Orlando, and Dallas. They're scary games, though. You can lose to anybody in this league, especially at their place.

We had just beaten the heck out of Minnesota at home, and I didn't know what to expect playing them again. We've always played well here, but after just beating them by 30, I wasn't sure how we were going to respond. But we won 104–93. It wasn't a solid win, but we did what we had to do. We were ready to play, but the Timberwolves played a much better game than they had at Portland and they hung around. We had a couple of chances to break it open, but we never could. Jerome had about 6 dunks. We'd get up

13, then they'd cut it back to 6 or 7. But at this time of year and on a trip like this, any win looks good.

April 4, 1991

Washington—Boy, did we have a strange game against the Bullets. We didn't play exceptionally well, and I thought we were a little tired. Bernard King wasn't playing for them but they had John Williams back. Pervis Ellison was much better than I had seen him play; he was really active, quick getting around us, getting to the basket and going to the boards.

It was a close game until the fourth quarter and then all heck broke loose. Danny Ainge blocked Williams's shot from behind, and I guess when Danny blocks your shot you have a right to complain—you just assume it was a foul. Danny claims it was a clean block, though. We were up by only 5 at the time, and Darrell Walker must have said the magic words to an official because he was tossed out in a second. He was gone in a real hurry.

About a minute later we had a fast break and Duck went up and dunked. Ellison came from behind him and gave him a little shove at the very end and was called for a foul. He should have just let him go. Ellison turned around and threw the ball to the official or at the official, and Steve Javie, who was the referee at the opposite end, came out of nowhere and threw Ellison out of the game.

Immediately there were only two happy people in the whole building because suddenly everything was going in our favor. I'm happy and Terry Porter is happy because he's standing at the free-throw line ready to shoot a whole bunch of free throws for technical fouls. I turn around and here comes Wes Unseld, the Washington coach—and that's a scary sight. He was really coming. They had just tossed two of his players and he was going to go, too.

Javie was very smart here. He just kept back-pedaling, trying to put people between him and Wes. Wes was really upset, and after he was kicked out and everything calmed down, we were up about 13 and the game was pretty much over. It suddenly went from a close game to an eruption.

It was our second straight win on this trip and eighth in a row overall. But more important, it was our fifth straight road win, and we were back on track. We're doing what we did earlier in the season—playing well against the good teams and well enough against the rest. We're playing very well in the fourth quarter, executing, defending, and re-bounding. When we get to the fourth quarter, we take over. We're getting that confidence back.

April 5, 1991

Orlando—I was frightened about this game because I think the Magic have a pretty good team. Scott Skiles had been playing well and the Magic are dangerous at home. Matt Guokas, I thought, has done a great job with that team. They beat some good teams—Golden State and Phoenix—on the road, and they had a plus record at home.

I was scared going into the game, and then when Clyde got kicked out of the game in the first half, I got really scared. We lost our poise in this game—not so much at the officials but at ourselves. It was one of the few times this season we did that.

Clyde got ejected so quickly. It came out of nowhere. They called a charge on him and he said something to Eddie Middleton, who gave him a technical. I thought Middleton should then have just told him, that's enough—get away from me. Instead, Clyde said something else and Middleton gave him another technical immediately. He's gone.

Then we got totally out of sync offensively. We were taking bad shots and then complaining to each other, arguing among ourselves. Somebody would say, hey, you're supposed to be there, and the other guy would say, I was there, move the ball. Everyone was involved in it.

We got frustrated. We were down about 10 at halftime, and I told our team, "You know, the first thing you've got to do is get back together. That's the first thing if you're going to win the game. You've got to regroup and quit complaining to each other. Or if someone says something to you, don't respond in a negative manner. Listen to it."

With Clyde out, everyone had to raise his level of play.

Under the circumstances, we went out and played one of our best quarters of the season. We outscored them 36–19 in the third period and went on to win by 17. Terry just took over the game. He came out and made five 3-pointers on them in the second half. He scored at will on Skiles. More important, Skiles got only two baskets the whole second half on Terry. Buck got every rebound, it seemed, and finished with 21 boards. Every time the ball went up, he was there. He was in a bubble and so was Terry. We just controlled the second half.

After the game I was going to reiterate what I had said at halftime, that the one thing we have never done as a group is start talking at each other or getting into that mode, but Buck picked up on it right away. He said that we can't be negative with each other. We have always been positive and we have to stay positive. He was saying that he wasn't going to put up with it.

Clyde was upset with himself about getting tossed. He knows it shouldn't have happened. I don't have to tell him I need him on the court, not in the locker room. The worst thing you can do, I think, is say anything about it. I kidded him about it instead. I told him, "You made fewer mistakes than I've ever seen you make in a game." He felt worse about it than anybody, and to say anything else to him about it would have been silly.

Something happened after the Orlando game that was significant, I think. We were in our locker room and had finished with the press. We were sitting around and someone turned on the San Antonio–Chicago game on the television.

Nobody left. They all just sat around and watched to see

who would win. I said something to Coop about Chicago; I was thinking, jeez, it would be nice if Chicago beats San Antonio because it would push San Antonio back a little bit in the Western Conference race.

Coop said no, we want San Antonio to win this game. We want them to push Chicago back. We want that best record in the league. That's what the attitude was.

They sat and watched the whole last quarter there in the locker room and the Bulls did lose. I could see there was a real focus to what this team wanted to accomplish. And I liked that a lot.

April 7, 1991

Dallas—We played another solid second half to win at Dallas, against a team that gave us fits all season. Cliff, as usual, just annihilated them. I think it's his quickness against their front line. He had been really struggling but he scored 22 on them. He'd been playing negatively, getting down on himself quickly if he missed his shots. He even asked to come out of the Minnesota game, which he never does. But he broke out of it in this game.

He's just too talented to stay in a slump for long. He made some great decisions in this game, passed the ball well, and got easier opportunities. We played a solid game and were very good in our halfcourt defense. Every time Rolando Blackman came off a pick we were right there. We forced their post-up people outside. We've won eleven in a row and seven straight on the road. We've won the four games we absolutely had to win, the ones everyone assumed we'd win, and we're set up for the final two games of the trip, which should be real tough games.

April 9, 1991

Houston—Everyone in Houston is talking about the Rockets. All you hear about is the Rockets and what a great team they are all of a sudden. We shot at the Summit the day before the game and I could tell we were going to play well. We had gotten those first games of the road trip out of the way, and it was like, okay, we took care of that and now we have two big challenges ahead of us.

At the start of the road trip I had figured if we won the first four games we'd be four, maybe even five games ahead of the Lakers. But the Lakers went into San Antonio and beat the Spurs, then went to Phoenix and beat the Suns, so our lead is just two and a half. We still have to play Houston and San Antonio on this trip, then go home and play the Lakers. If they beat us, they'd have the season series on us and only need to tie us to win the division.

But I told the guys, well, the Lakers went on the road and won, and then San Antonio, after losing at home to the Lakers, went out and beat Milwaukee, Chicago, and Minnesota on the road. If we're going to win it, we're going to have to do it ourselves and win it on the road—which is the way it should be anyway. It's the way we wanted it.

We played another solid defensive game at Houston and beat them 103–93. We went out and played with a purpose. They were sky-high for us. Sky-high. You could even see it while they were shooting lay-ups. It was as if this were the final test for them. They had a four-game road trip coming up to end the season, and this was going to set them off. They came out and jumped us right from the start.

Usually when they do that to us, it's hard for us to get back into the game. They're a better running team at home than they are on the road, and they play with so much more confidence there. Their guards started the game off making shots, but we had talked about playing soft on their guards, giving them outside shots. If someone gets on a roll, you have to move up on that guy, but we feel all their guards are inconsistent.

Sleepy Floyd and Vernon Maxwell shoot about 40 percent. Maxwell shoots a ton of 3s, but he doesn't shoot a good percentage. He made some to open the game, so Clyde moved out on him a little. We didn't panic, though. We just had to keep playing, to weather the storm and stay close at the half. Then they jumped on us at the start of the third quarter again.

We had to call a time-out, but again there was no panic. We just kept playing and stuck with our game plan. We didn't want to give them anything easy, and we wanted them to be an outside-shooting team. Soon we caught a run and turned the game around. We got Olajuwon in foul trouble, which we almost always do. If we move and we're active, he'll get out of position and he reacts.

He has trouble playing Duck, too, because Duck makes him play inside and outside. He reaches and he does some things that draw fouls that other big guys won't do. He goes for steals all the time, even against guards. Because he's so quick he gets those steals sometimes, but he picks up fouls, too. He went out in the third period with foul trouble and we started getting to the basket. When he's in the game, let's face it, he's hell on wheels. He's so quick. You can penetrate, make a great move, draw him to you, kick it to the open man, and he still gets back to block the shot. If you don't take your shot right away, he'll block it. But with him out of the game, the basket opened up for us. The same thing happened for us when we played them later on.

I think it said something for us as a team that we had gone through that great early-season run, then went down for a while, then really responded. We've matured as a team and we didn't panic. And now we're back. You can just see it. We aren't getting too high for these games, either; we're just preparing ourselves. We're playing with emotion but not too much so, and we're still relaxed. It's just a quiet confidence.

I felt good about this game because everyone had been talking so much about Houston and they had been beating everyone. And for us to go in there and keep our streak alive was great. We can now do no worse than go home with a two-game lead over the Lakers.

April 10, 1991

San Antonio—I didn't think I needed to say a whole lot
going into this game, but I brought up the fact that we've
lost two games in a row to them and they do an awful lot
of talking about us. They don't seem to give us credit when
we beat them. And I think we give them a lot of credit. I
think they're a very good team and maybe the talking is just
their way of showing us they're good.

We came into town and the papers were saying the Blazers
are coming into town with twelve wins in a row, eight of
them on the road, but the Spurs are cool. All we have to do
is play our game and we'll win, they said. We know we can
beat them, they said. I didn't have to say a whole lot to my
team. But the last thing I told them before we went out on
the court is that we owe them. We owe them. We lost a
home game to them and we should have beaten them the
last time we were at their place, but we didn't.

We knew they'd be ready to play, we knew they would
spurt, and we knew their crowd would go crazy when they
did. And we knew we would weather it when it happened,
just as we did at Houston. We wanted to play a solid
game, stay close, and have a chance to win in the fourth
quarter.

That's just what we did. We beat them 105–100. We had
a good lead in the fourth quarter, they came back at us, but
Jerome hit a really big shot down the stretch and we put
them away. I played all eleven men I had in the first half,
and Danny Young hit a huge 3-pointer. Danny Young,
Danny Ainge, Alaa, and Walter kept us in the game in the
second quarter when we had some foul trouble with our
starters. We defended them well all night. We played smart.

We made the decision this week that we were going to
try to play Walter and Danny Ainge at the same time. We
haven't been able to find Walter a lot of quality minutes to
this point. Using them at the same time is about the only
way I can get him out on the floor for some playing time.
It's going to take Danny away from where he plays best, at

off-guard. But if we're going to get Walter ready for the playoffs, he needs some minutes.

San Antonio jumped on us at the start of the third quarter, but Clyde took over and made two incredible drives that only the great players make. He made one where he was hit, threw the ball up off his hip, spun it off the board, and it went in. Then Cliff made a sensational pass to Clyde for a basket with about four minutes to go. Still, they came back at us, and Jerome—who had been 1 for 7 from the field to that point—knocked down an open jumper with 1:20 to go and that cinched it.

I'm not sure if Jerome would have made that shot two years ago, especially when he was having a tough game. He usually shoots well when he's in a rhythm, but he was really struggling in this game. A couple of years ago, he wouldn't even have taken this shot, he would have tried to drive it. This time, though, it was nothing but net and it broke their backs.

It was an unbelievable win. All those teams were making runs at us, and we responded by beating Houston and San Antonio on the road, teams that were trying to win their own division. It was the kind of thing the Lakers or Boston or Detroit would have done in the past. They go out and win games that everyone figures they're going to lose. I think we left a lot of people around the league shaking their heads.

We couldn't do that last year, when I think we snuck up on some teams. But this trip . . . I talked with Geoff Petrie beforehand about how good it would be to just get four out of six. But we got a sweep and we're really on a roll.

And now we go home to play the Lakers.

April 13, 1991

Portland—It's a funny thing, but going into this game I felt very little pressure. I felt sure we were going to win the division. This would be the perfect way to do it, too. We wanted to beat them so we could win the season series from them, win the Pacific Division from them, keep the winning streak alive, and do all of it on national television at last. It was the first time NBC had been to Portland all year long. And it was only the second time we'd been on the network all season.

The hype around this game made it seem like the next eruption of Mt. St. Helens. But we were confident and ready. We knew it was going to be a heck of a game because it usually is when we play the Lakers. But some people think the only rivalries around the league are the ones that TV perceives as rivalries. I've said all along that if they want to have a good game on TV, they ought to put the Phoenix-Portland games on for the last two years. Every game we play with them has been a great one.

The networks get tied into those old rivalries involving Philadelphia, Boston, New York, and Chicago. Well, we've had better games out here with Phoenix and the Lakers than any of them. But really, it's Michael Jordan, Magic Johnson, Larry Bird, in the New York market. There's such an Eastern flavor. We understand that. But we don't particularly like it.

I think people get tired of watching the same teams all the time. It helps when someone new comes along, like Detroit did a couple of years ago. We surprised people last year and won 59 games and were as good as Detroit on the road in the regular season. They beat us in the Finals, but everyone was predicting we would be one of the teams in the thick of it this year. So wouldn't you think we would be a pretty good draw?

But getting back to the Laker game, we were really confident and relaxed, and Clyde set the tone. He's not one of the top 3-point shooters in the world, but I don't know how many times he's made big ones. He hit a couple in the first quarter that really got us going. Everybody was in tune. We got way up on them in the third quarter, but I have to give Sam Perkins and Byron Scott credit—they got their team all the way back into the game. Scott just caught fire, as he has so many times against us over the years.

But Clyde went back into the game and he was unbelievable. He rose up in a big game on national TV and just carried us. He made a big shot over Perkins down the stretch and we won it 118–113.

It was the type of thing Magic or Jordan does. When the game is on the line, they respond. And I was so pleased for Clyde because I think it meant a lot to him that he responded with the division title on the line. It was fitting he was able to do that. It capped a tremendous run for us.

Jake O'Donnell officiated the game, as he did for a few other games down the stretch of the season, with no problems at all. His problem with our team just seemed to fade away with the season. The fans didn't even seem to react to him in any big way. I'm glad that's died down because he's one of the top-rated officials and we're going to get him in some big games during the playoffs.

Before the Laker game, somebody from the front office came into the locker room with a big box and said, "These are the T-shirts." Mike Shimensky looked at him kind of funny, and even though it didn't involve me, I asked Mike, "What T-shirts?" The guy said they were Pacific Division Champion T-shirts, and that if we won the game, they wanted the players to wear them afterward.

I told Mike to put them in storage. Nobody had said a word to me about that. I said, number one, we haven't won, and number two, if we do win it, that's not what we're trying to accomplish. I didn't even know if the players wanted them or not.

I do know one thing, though. When I got home that day after the game, I couldn't quite believe what we had done this season.

April 14, 1991

Portland—We beat Orlando 139–119 to officially wrap up the best record in the league. It rendered the final three games on our schedule rather meaningless.

Roger Sabrowski asked me if I wanted to give the T-shirts

out. We really had nothing left to play for the rest of the season, except to keep our streak alive. So I said to the players after the game, "They brought these T-shirts in last night and I don't know if you guys want them or not."

Clyde said, "That's not the T-shirt we want." Buck said, "Just burn them. We don't want them." Then Duck said, "Hey, I want them. I've got a couple of people I want to give them to."

Everyone laughed. And everyone took some. The guys have them and they'll wear them. I took a couple of them home myself. But it wasn't the T-shirt we wanted. That's okay. I don't have any problem with anyone making T-shirts up. We're proud of what we did.

I really think that the Laker era of dominating the West is over. I know they still have a very good team, but we played better than they did all season long. I think with this season, we have finally put them behind us. At least as far as the regular season is concerned.

April 21, 1991

Phoenix—We finished up with easy wins over Houston and Sacramento at home, passing the ball as well as we had all season long. We could easily have let down, but we pushed the win streak all the way up to 16. We didn't just go through the motions; we continued to play hard. We wanted to run it out all the way to the end, but we got murdered at Phoenix on the final day of the season in a game that was a lot more important to them than it was to us.

One thing that really disappointed us that last weekend was that our game with Phoenix, originally scheduled to be on national television, was scratched at the last minute in favor of Detroit and Chicago, a game that had no effect on anything.

We have a 16-game win streak and Phoenix needed to win the game for playoff seeding. But NBC didn't show it. That astounded me. About this time, too, we found out our

first four games in the first round of the playoffs were not
going to be on NBC, either. I mean, I couldn't believe they
were going to have four games that first weekend on NBC
and we weren't in any of them.

They said that the Lakers vs. Houston is a better matchup.
I want to take a step back, because last year we were playing
Dallas in the first round and everyone thought that was the
best first-round matchup of all, and they didn't put those
games on CBS; they put the Lakers on against Houston, the
eighth-seeded team in the West. To me, our team deserved
to be on. Our players deserved that recognition. I think it
helps your players to get on national television once in a
while. They deserve that when they compile the league's
best record.

I can understand promoting the players individually, but
why and how does NBC decide who it's going to promote?
Why isn't Clyde Drexler one of the guys they promote? Why
is it Isiah Thomas or David Robinson? This is why we never
get a starter in the all-star game—because the network
doesn't promote our guys because, I guess, we're in a small
market.

I guess I undertand that this is all about money. But I
can't help wishing they'd remember that the ''product''
they're selling is basketball. And this year, over the course
of the season, we played the best basketball in the league. I
don't know what it takes to be the marquee team, but when
you compile the best record in the league, you deserve some
recognition.

But the chance for that is ahead. In the playoffs.

Seattle

April 24, 1991

Portland—Why do they give everybody three or four days to prepare for the first round of the playoffs? It's only a short series. Later, between rounds of crucial seven-game series, you often get only one or two days to get ready. It would be nice to have three days between each round—wishful thinking.

I picked up the newspaper this morning, *The Oregonian,* and it's just packed with playoff stuff. There was an entire special section, in addition to the regular sports section. I don't know, with everything going on, if I'll get a chance to read much of it. There's just so much coverage.

Even though we've had a hell of a year people are taking the position that if we don't win the championship, forget it. I think we have a great chance, barring injury, of going all the way. A great chance. But if it doesn't happen, we aren't the worst people in the world. We have deficiencies. Our strengths outweigh them, but we have some that can crop up and cause us to lose a couple of games.

Putting aside the hype, there is a tremendous amount of genuine excitement. I'm very excited. This is a great time of the season.

We aren't supposed to lose to Seattle, which is the eighth-seeded team in the Western Conference. No eighth seed has ever beaten a top seed. And so I can't imagine the pressure getting any tougher at any point of the playoffs than it is right now. We're just not supposed to lose to these guys.

But Seattle in a five-game series is not a comfortable proposition.

I'm almost certain that the first-round series will someday be changed to a best-of-seven series. I've never understood why these should be short series. The league takes a big chance that a good team can get eliminated in the first round simply because of the format of the series. If you lose one of those first two games at home in a five-game series, you just don't have any time to get back in the series.

It happened to Utah a few years ago against Golden State. And it happened to us one year against Utah. You lose one of those first two home games, and then you immediately have to get a win on the other team's homecourt. Panic can set in and you just don't have a chance to get back into it.

I've closed our practices this week and come under some criticism by the media because of it. I wanted the team to focus in on Seattle because with all the personnel they've changed throughout the season—Ricky Pierce for Dale Ellis, Benoit Benjamin for Olden Polynice, and Eddie Johnson for Xavier McDaniel—they pose a different problem for us than other teams. I'm not concerned about what they do offensively. It's how they defend.

They can take us out of our offense with their double-teaming and fronting of the low post. I want the players to concentrate on that, and I don't want them being distracted during practices. I want a serious tone set for our first game.

I closed our game-day shootaround, too. In the shoot-arounds during the playoffs we normally get them out of bed in the morning, get them thinking about the game, and just shoot around a little bit. We've already talked about how we'll defend them and what we'll do against them on offense. But I learned last year that if you don't close your shoot-around in the playoffs, you set a bad precedent for later in the playoffs.

If you start getting the games telecast, then you get the TV commentators showing up and they haven't been around all year, so they want to come to the shootarounds. Not only them, but the technicians are all around, setting up. You've let all those people in so you really have to let everyone else in, too—all the print and electronic reporters. It's just a whole lot easier not to let anyone in. For forty-five minutes we can relax, shoot around a little, and talk in a group if we want to.

I don't understand why all the reporters feel they have to be there to watch our guys shoot the ball and chat with them. But they do. NBC always wants to be there, and I have to say they've been great about respecting our wishes. But if you let them in, I think you have to let everyone else in, too. Our beat reporters have been with us all year, and I can't keep them out and let NBC in. It's easier just to have it closed to everyone.

We've been a relaxed team all week. I feel good about this series. We're confident, yet we've been intense and receptive in practice. I think we're going to be okay. But I don't expect it to be as easy as a lot of the media and fans think it will be. Seattle could give us trouble.

April 26, 1991

Portland—Jerome was unbelievable at the start of the game. He was all over the court. Eddie Johnson, whom they picked up from Phoenix, was doing his job, keeping them in the game with his shooting.

Johnson scored 25 of his 33 points in the second half, but Clyde was even better; he made 14 of 22 from the field, 9 of 10 from the foul line, and scored 27 of his 39 in the second half. He also had 9 assists, 7 rebounds, and 3 steals. He just took over and we won 110–102. He had 19 in the fourth quarter.

Seattle didn't go inside as much as we thought they would, probably because Johnson was on such a roll and they were looking for him. Then Pierce came in and they were looking for him, trying to get him going. The way they play, sometimes it's hard to get the right mix of going inside and outside.

They do so much defensive switching. We talked about not looking for the first guy in our offense coming up, but rather looking for the guy at the basket. And then when they fronted our post men, we wanted to swing the ball and look inside. Then we wanted to pound the boards. We did it in spots during the game, but we didn't do it consistently.

Still, we did it enough to win when Clyde stepped up and took over. We never trailed in the second half, but we didn't ever get much of a lead, either. We couldn't shake them.

I was a little shaken, though, when I heard after the game about something that happened prior to it. My daughter Kathy, who is a sophomore at the University of Portland, and some of her friends came up with the idea of making up T-shirts that looked a little like our uniforms, except that instead of saying "Portland" on the front they said "Porterland." They figured they would make a little money from it.

I wasn't real excited about it because of the position I'm in, but I was busy preparing for the playoffs and didn't give it a lot of thought. She wasn't too involved in it; she helped them design it and then she wore one around.

They sold some of the shirts to a store and they were popular on campus at the college. Before the game they were going to try to sell some of them near the coliseum. If I had known that, I would have stopped them, but I didn't hear about it. They were all caught up in it and it seemed pretty harmless at the time.

They had about five or six shirts with them and were out in front of the coliseum trying to get rid of them, and before they knew it, they were arrested. They were handcuffed—

which I don't think was necessary—and taken to a room inside the arena.

The authorities had a major operation going on to curb the illegal selling of merchandise. There is some rule, one that the kids had no knowledge of at the time, that you can go two or three blocks from the coliseum and sell things, but you can't do it any closer than that. Plus, you're supposed to have a license. They were trying to stop scalpers and people selling items that weren't authorized by the team.

They came in and got Mary Kay, who was already in her seat, and she had to deal with it just prior to the game. They issued a citation and Kathy was given a court date. The media hasn't heard anything about it yet, but I'm sure they will. I'm a little concerned about how it will be handled.

April 27, 1991

Portland—In preparing for the second game of the series, I feel good about our situation. I think Seattle played well in the first game, but I know we can play much better. Cliff and Danny Ainge did not have good games, and Terry wasn't real good, either. If they step up their games, we're going to win the second game. I know we can play better, but I don't know if Seattle can.

April 28, 1991

Portland—The game was tense, but Terry and Danny Ainge came to the rescue. The Sonics still didn't go inside as much as we thought they would, and I think in the fourth quarter, when we jumped on them, they got tired.

We won 115–106 and we did just what we talked about doing. We wanted to keep pressure on them and we felt we were going to have two or three surges. They kept coming back at us until the fourth period, when I don't think they had anything left.

We have our 2–0 lead, and now they're going to have to beat us three in a row if they're going to win. It feels good to go into that third game at Seattle with a 2–0 lead. The only thing that bothered me a little bit was that we had a 20-point lead and allowed them to close it down with some easy baskets at the end of the game.

April 29, 1991

Seattle—We feel we have a good chance to win tomorrow for a number of reasons. I think there's a little doubt in their minds that they can beat us. And they haven't established anything around the basket at all.

I know they're going to come out in the first half and throw everything they have at us. We have to fight through that and stay close. But if we're in the game as the fourth quarter approaches, we have an excellent chance to win. I think if we're still in it at that point, they may fade away.

The other factor is that they have not sold out the game and a lot of our fans have bought tickets and are making the three-hour drive up here. It's going to be like that earlier game at Tacoma, I think. If we have a big portion of the crowd with us, it's going to have a bigger impact as the game goes along.

April 30, 1991

Seattle—We did stay close all the way. We did what we wanted to do right up until the final minute of the game. We didn't play a great game, but we played pretty well.

But some little things, as they so often do, drive you crazy. The videotape of the game is going through the machine right now, and it drives me crazy to see all the little things that influence the final outcome. After winning six straight games against them through the season, almost every one of them decided down the stretch, we let this one get away. In almost unbelievable—for us—fashion.

We shot 54.1 percent from the floor and lost because we were outrebounded 43–31 and made only 18 of 28 from the foul line while they were making 28 of 34. We were up 22–13 late in the first quarter, but got outscored 18–2 over a six-minute stretch and trailed 54–45 at halftime.

But we opened the second half with a 17–2 spurt that shot us into the lead again. Seattle led 79–77 going into the final quarter, but we opened the period with a 9–0 run that I thought might put them away. But it didn't. They tied it at 87 and it was tight the rest of the way.

We had a 96–91 lead with 3:06 to go, but the Sonics came back. The lead was 2 with under a minute to go, and Terry had the ball when Benoit Benjamin came to double-team him. Terry picked up his dribble, which he shouldn't have done; with his dribble, he could have just busted past him to the basket. But Benjamin just engulfed him, and instead of getting a foul call, it was called a jump ball.

We got the tip, but it ran more time off the clock and we missed our shot. We ran our 2-out play but they doubled Clyde, and he gave it to Terry—who was wide open. He could have shot, but he saw Buck going down the lane. Buck was open briefly, but someone slid over and picked him up and he missed a tough finger roll. Instead of being 4 ahead, we were 2 up and they had the ball.

Derrick McKey tied it by making a difficult shot with 38.3 seconds to go, but we got a terrific play from Duck to take the lead. After we missed two shots, Kevin reached up with his left hand and guided a tip-in off the backboard and in with 21.7 seconds to go to lift us into a 99–97 lead.

They had no time-outs left and had their defensive team on the floor. I was worried about only one guy shooting the ball—and that was Sedale Threatt, who was having a great game. Sure enough, Threatt got the ball with the clock ticking down and took it to the top of the 3-point circle. I believe Danny Ainge thought he was close enough to affect the shot, but Threatt went up and knocked down a 3-point field goal to give them a 100–99 lead with four seconds left. Instead of being tied, we're down by a point all of a sudden.

Still, that's plenty of time to get up a good shot. By this time, the arena is in an uproar, and our fans are holding their own. It was the most amazing atmosphere for a playoff game I've ever seen. The place was split about fifty-fifty, at least noisewise, and it was total bedlam.

We called a time-out and set up a play with Ainge taking the ball out of bounds. Once we got back out on the floor I was tempted to call a time-out to make sure we all knew what we were going to do because the way they were lined up on defense, we were going to get the ball to Clyde or Terry with a great opportunity. But if you call another time-out, they might come back and line up differently, so I let it go.

Nobody was guarding Terry. They were guarding the outside completely. Clyde made the decision to come to the ball. If Terry had come high, he'd have had nobody on him at all. Little decisions. Still, when Clyde came to the ball, he was open, and I swear, if he catches it, he dunks the ball because there's nobody there to stop him.

But Danny bounced the pass instead of throwing it all the way in the air. That gave Gary Payton a chance to catch up with it and he picked it off. They scored at the buzzer and we lost 102–99.

It scared the heck out of me. I was shocked. I can't believe we lost the game that way. We had control of the game and it was the kind of game we had won all season—especially against them.

It was a very tough loss to take.

May 1, 1991

Seattle—We have a couple of days to practice, and what I want to do is not dwell on what happened in the last game. We not only lost our chance to sweep the series, I think we gave them some confidence. They're a young team and they weren't quite sure they could beat us.

But we gave them some life.

They established Benjamin around the basket in the third game. He went 14 for 14 from the foul line. I'm not as concerned as everyone else seems to be with the four or five baskets he made from the floor; they were from ten to twelve feet, and I'm not sure that we wouldn't give him those every time. What bothered me was that we allowed him offensive rebounds and let him get in close to the basket, where we fouled him. He's in his first playoff series ever, and I hate the thought of his gaining too much confidence.

May 2, 1991

Seattle—We came out and played a poor game and they played a good game. When that happens, there isn't much question who is going to win. They stuck us 101–89 and tied the series 2–2.

Again, I thought we had control of the game. They had us down 52–44 at the half, but we played a strong third quarter and led them 76–72 going into the fourth period. But our inability to make free throws cost us any chance of winning the game. We hit only 20 of 39 for the game, an embarrassing 51.3 percent. And to make matters worse, we were 9 for 21 in the second half and only 3 for 10 in the fourth quarter.

We defended them well in the fourth quarter, but when we came to the other end, they fouled us and we missed the free throws. Or we would miss lay-ups. That went on for a while before they suddenly started scoring and they just took off. We couldn't survive missing that many free throws.

Once more they just crushed us on the boards. I guess there was no way we were going to win this game. We just flat-out got beat.

I went into the locker room after the game and didn't say anything at all about the game. I didn't talk about the rebounds or the missed free throws. All I said was that we didn't play well. But I wanted to get to my players before the media did.

I knew all the talk when the media came in would be about how the pressure is now on us. No eighth seed had ever beaten a number one seed. Seattle had nothing to lose and we had everything to lose.

I talked to the players about trying to put games three and four out of their minds. I want them to put into perspective what kind of team they are. We won 63 games. We just went through a 16-game winning streak. We've been through pressure situations and tough games before. I want them to have positive thoughts in their minds. We racked up the best record in the league and played hard all season to do it—for just this reason.

We're going home for game five. They have to come to our place again. They have never gone through anything like what they're going to have to go through on Saturday.

You don't want to dwell on the fact that you have to win this game. What you want in your mind is to remember what makes you good. We have to play aggressively and with emotion. If we play the way we're capable of playing, we'll have some fun. If we play uptight, scared, or frightened of the consequences, then we won't play well. We have to play to win the game—not play not to lose. I don't want us to play scared.

The news of Kathy's arrest hit the papers today, and tomorrow is her court date. It made the front page of a paper in San Diego and was picked up all over the country. "Coach's Daughter Arrested" makes a nice headline, but it really wasn't that big a deal. A college kid getting busted for selling a T-shirt doesn't seem that important, with everything else going on in the world.

I think more than anything it emphasized to her that because of my position, she is very identifiable.

May 3, 1991

Portland—For game five, we decided to change our game plan. We feel we're best when we're most aggressive. Sometimes you get caught in situations where you get indecisive. And we have to be active. We played their outside people pretty well, but when they started going inside, we were hesitant. We didn't know if we wanted to double-team or not. We were unsure.

For tomorrow's game, we said the hell with it. If a guy catches the ball inside, go after him. We'll rotate to the next guy and the next guy. We'll make them make four passes if we have to. We hadn't put a lot of pressure on the ball because they have some guys like Payton and Nate McMillan who haven't shot the ball well from the outside. They're both penetraters, and by sagging off them we've cut off their lanes to the basket, but we've lost some of that emotion that makes us effective.

It hit home while we were looking at tape that we've been standing around and letting them make passes. So we changed. We decided if we were going to make a mistake, it was going to be a mistake of aggression, not a mistake of being passive.

What we had been doing defensively was working, when we did it correctly. But it cost us some of our aggressiveness.

We decided to have our guards go down the floor and pick up their guards a little quicker—get all over them. We hadn't done that the whole series.

We are going to play their game. If Duck thinks he can jump around Benjamin and front him, he's going to do it. But he can't do it unless we get pressure on the ball.

Kathy went to court and was given a small fine and told not to do it again. I think she understands that by now. She also realizes she's in the public eye and everything she does is going to be magnified either way—positive or negative.

I think our other three children learned the same lesson. They were astounded their sister got so much attention from the incident.

May 4, 1991

Portland—We were down 23–19 in the first quarter when Danny Ainge came in and made a couple of long jump shots. It sent us off on an 11–0 run that helped us take command of the game. We led 63–43 at halftime and had a 104–74 edge with 7:55 to go.

We were so aggressive that even when we were down early in the game, I felt it was going to turn around and go our way. As soon as Danny made those two shots, we got even more aggressive.

I looked at the Sonics and they seemed a little bit flustered. Their best chance was to get off to a good start and stay ahead. I knew that if we got any kind of a run going, our crowd was going to explode. Then our guys would feed off that and get even more aggressive. And I felt that somewhere during the game that would happen. But even in the early going, when they were making some shots, Seattle did not look confident to me.

I took the starters out late in the game and we got outscored 26–9 over the last six minutes so the final score was only 119–107. I wasn't real pleased about that.

We missed three or four shots and went to the basket a couple of times and didn't get calls. Then we had some guys pouting because they hadn't gotten into the game early enough. Before we knew it they'd scored 10 or 12 points in about a minute and ten seconds.

After the game I congratulated everyone and we talked about what a great win it was. We had played well on national TV. I felt good about our team. It wasn't just that we had won but that we had done what great teams do. It was something I'd seen Detroit do. We turned our aggression and defense up so high there was nothing the other team could do.

But we played too hard to give up so many easy points late in the game. I feel for the guys who don't get into the game until the end, but I don't like some of the attitudes I saw. You don't have to knock guys into the stands when they have open shots, but you have to challenge the plays.

This team is bigger than anybody's attitude. I have guys like Walter Davis, who has been an all-star in this league, and when I asked him to go in with three minutes to go, he was off the bench and into the game in a second. And he does whatever it takes. I wasn't upset at him; he missed three wide-open shots, but I hope he takes them every time he gets them. I have no problem with guys missing shots.

But it's a question of effort. It irritated me and I let the players know it did. It kind of put a damper on the game and I wanted to let them know I didn't want it to happen again.

But it was a great win for us, just the same. And I finished off my talk with the players by telling them that. We really showed how good we were.

It was a pleasure to watch the way we went out and handled the situation. It was a tremendous accomplishment because I'm not sure there's ever been a better eighth-seeded team than the Sonics. You finish with the best record in the league and end up playing a team this good in the first round—that's a tough assignment.

They had added Johnson, Pierce, and Benjamin to their team in the last two months of the season. If they'd had those three guys all year, I can tell you for sure they wouldn't have been the number eight seed. I was more concerned about having to play Seattle or Golden State than Houston. You know what you're going to get from Houston. Golden State, as San Antonio found out, is so unconventional. And Seattle is the same way. They do things differently from other teams, especially on defense, and that makes it difficult in a short series.

The Spurs lost to the Warriors in the first round. They got beat at home to start the series and just couldn't get it back home for the fifth game. I really believe you'll see those first-round series changed to seven-game series next season. It probably took a team such as San Antonio losing in the first round to make it happen. The league, and particularly NBC, didn't want to lose San Antonio and David Robinson in the first round. In those five-game series you just don't have a lot of time to make adjustments, and you lose one game and you're in trouble.

Our advantage in this series is that we won the first two games at home, which San Antonio didn't do. If San Antonio had had a seven-game series and could have come home for a game five and won, then gone back to Golden State for a game six, it would have given them one more shot at winning on the road. Panic would probably not have set in and they may have won game three or four at Oakland.

Golden State took away David Robinson on the inside, and the Spurs are a little like us in that they're a passing-game team and not a great outside-shooting team. Golden State forced them to shoot outside. Even with Robinson, San Antonio doesn't have a strong post-up player. Robinson is more of a slasher, sort of like some of our guys. They don't have anyone who is going to pound you inside. Terry Cummings is more of a jump shooter. Golden State hurt them with the small lineup. But I don't expect them to hurt the Lakers with it in the second round. I expect Los Angeles not to have too much trouble. We have to play Utah while Los Angeles meets the Warriors. We may end up playing Golden State, but I doubt it.

The Lakers have Sam Perkins and James Worthy to go to. And Magic Johnson won't allow them to do things they did against San Antonio. He'll spread the court and expose them. If they give Byron Scott those wide-open jumpers they gave San Antonio, he'll make them. Golden State's defense is susceptible. The Warriors were able to double-team David Robinson and get away with it. The Lakers will do a better job of spacing the court and exposing that defensive tactic. Magic will get the ball to the open shooters and the Lakers have people who can make those shots.

Plus, it's a seven-game series. The Warriors can come into the Forum and steal a game and it won't be the end of the world. The Lakers are too smart to panic. They've been through it all so many times. I think they'll just pound them inside, and if they have to, they can play with a small lineup, too.

I hope that playing a pretty good team in the first round is an advantage to us. We had to play well. And we're going to have to play well again in the next series because Utah is an outstanding team.

Utah

May 6, 1991

Portland—The key to this series is how we're going to play offensively. I believe that we're going to be able to defend them well enough most of the time. I think we can limit what they'll try to do in most of the games. They will be good, though; Karl Malone and John Stockton will get theirs.

There are two keys. If we play well offensively, moving the ball and moving their people around, we're going to get some shots at the basket and Mark Eaton will not be a factor. If we don't move the ball and move the defense, then we become a stagnant team and we'll be in trouble against them. The other key is how well they shoot from the outside. I'm talking mostly about Stockton, Thurl Bailey, and Blue Edwards. Jeff Malone will make his shots; I think you have to expect that. But if their other guys make outside shots when you double down, they can really give you some problems.

We have to attack Karl Malone at our offensive end. We have to attack Stockton, too. We have to make them work hard and use up some energy at the defensive end.

Stockton has a hard time getting through screens so we have to get Terry involved; we're going to try to run him off a lot of screens. Terry has to be the aggressor. Whenever we've beaten them, Terry's had good offensive games. When we haven't beaten them, he hasn't gotten enough shots.

It's an interesting series. In most of our games during the season, one club or the other was without key players.

There are some classic matchups in this series. You've got Karl Malone against Buck Williams—perhaps the best offensive power forward in the game against probably the best defensive power forward. That's a terrific matchup. And you've got Stockton vs. Porter—a couple of virtual unknowns when they came into the league. No one predicted either one would be the player he's become. They're both tremendous players and tremendous people, too.

Then you have Clyde vs. Jeff Malone. I don't think people realize how good Jeff Malone is. He was an all-star type of player at Washington and he's a very good defender, too.

Then you have Duck vs. Eaton. Eaton has given Duck a lot of trouble over the years, but Duck can also give him headaches. Duck's gotten better against him as the years have gone along. Duck is probably a tremendous key to the series. If he shoots the ball well, he can really hurt them by pulling Eaton out away from the basket. If Eaton becomes a factor in this series, we're going to have trouble beating them. If he just plays a normal game and is not a big factor, we probably have a pretty good chance to win.

My biggest worry is that Buck will get in foul trouble early and won't be allowed to be as tough with Malone as Malone is with him. If you can't do that with Malone, you can't set the tone and he completely dictates the game. You're never going to be able to stop Karl Malone. But it's important you make him work for everything he gets.

We'll rotate Mark Bryant, Cliff, and Alaa on him if we have to. But obviously, the best guy on our team to guard him is Buck because he's smart and knows what he can and can't do. He doesn't worry about how many points his man gets. He'll just keep banging away.

May 7, 1991

Portland—We didn't play as well as we were capable of playing in the Seattle series, and I was a little concerned about this first game against the Jazz.

But we played pretty well defensively and we shut them down. We pretty much controlled it. We dominated them on the boards, with Clyde getting 15 rebounds and Jerome 13. They never got on track, and probably the big reason was that Karl Malone was only 8 for 24 from the field and got to the foul line only 7 times. If he does that, we're going to beat them most of the time.

Stockton had a really good game, but even though we were up only 5 at the half, I felt we were in control. We had a big third quarter and ended up winning 117–97.

Clyde made a big play in the third quarter. We were leading only 68–66 with 5:32 to go in the period when he went to the basket and got hit by two people. No foul was called on the play but he took a hard fall. When he got up, we called a 20-second time-out and Clyde got that look in his eye. Look out when he gets that look because he's going to take off.

He just exploded. He was everywhere on defense, and then he was feeding people or knocking down his shots at the other end. Before I knew it we were up 78–68 and on our way.

They shot only 39 percent and we shot 50. It reminded me a lot of the first game of our series in 1988 when we really handled them but then lost the next three games, and the five-game series. You never want to think that, because this is a different team, but I did anyway.

May 8, 1991

Portland—I am very afraid that Karl Malone is going to come out with a monster game in game two. He was only 8 for 24 in the first game and he's going to come out and make up for it.

As much attention as the games are getting in Portland, they're being rivaled for the spotlight by something off the court. Amid the playoff fervor a man decided to open a restaurant not far from the coliseum and he called it the Rip City Diner.

Rip City is a term our broadcaster, Bill Schonely, began using right from the first season the Blazers were in Portland. When a guy swishes a shot from the outside, The Schonz, as we call him, is likely to say, "Rip City."

The Schonz has been with the franchise since day one. People identify with the team through him. He's as much a celebrity in Portland as the players, a lot like the way Vin Scully is synonymous with the Dodgers in southern California, or Chick Hearn is with the Lakers. Bill is always the first person to try to pick me up after a loss. He is very loyal. I can't imagine a Blazer game without him on the sideline.

But our front office felt the use of *Rip City* was trademark infringement and sent the owner of the place a letter telling him he had no right to use it as the name of the establishment. The Blazers, the letter said, own *Rip City*.

Well, the timing on that was definitely not the best. The owner of the place went to the media and the public was overwhelmingly in support of him. Soon the whole town was up in arms and the organization came off looking pretty bad. Meanwhile, we're in the middle of the playoffs and this is becoming a major thing. Our front office had no idea it would develop into something like this.

There were editorials in the papers and on television, and everywhere you went someone was cracking a joke about the Blazers owning some kind of generic word such as *foul* or *basketball.*

The whole thing just exemplifies the feelings the people

in this area have for their basketball team. The city, the fans, the whole state—they regard this team as theirs. It doesn't belong to the Blazer organization—it belongs to everyone. People have been making up Rip City signs and, yes, T-shirts for years. They feel it's their slogan, not just the organization's.

It didn't distract our players at all. They didn't get involved in it. But everywhere you go around town people are talking about the owner of this place and his battle against the organization. It just shows how wildly things get blown out of proportion here when they involve the Blazers. The team has had to retract its position and tell the guy to go ahead and call his place the Rip City Diner. But the story is still hanging around.

It's probably difficult for people elsewhere around the country to understand this kind of attention. I know in southern California it just wouldn't be a big deal. But it shows the way the people around here identify with their team. And I do mean *their* team.

May 9, 1991

Portland—Before the game, we talked a little about that Utah series in '88. I reminded the players who were here about what happened, how we gave the series right back to them in game two.

But I didn't have to worry. We just dominated this game from the start. Terry and Clyde and some of the other guys had been around for that other Utah series, and I think they remembered what happened, too. Everyone was really in tune. For three quarters.

Going into the fourth quarter, Jeff Malone was the only guy hurting us. Karl Malone was okay, not the monster I'd feared. But at the start of the fourth quarter, with a 94–71 lead, we started to relax defensively and we began to put them on the free-throw line. Again and again we put them at the free-throw line. The game was a rout, and then suddenly, they were shooting free throws every time down the court. The clock was stopping all the time and we began to struggle. They just kept coming at us, and when we didn't foul them, they made every shot.

Before we knew it, it was anyone's ball game down the stretch. Karl Malone went to the foul line 20 times in the second half, made 19—a playoff record—and finished with 40 points. Finally, we ran our 2-out with the score tied, and Clyde hit Terry with a bullet pass for a lay-up with 3.6 seconds to play. They got the ball to Stockton, who attempted a 3-pointer, but it missed and we had a 118–116 win.

Many people were concerned because we blew a big lead. But a lot of factors entered into that, including our relaxing too much at both ends of the court. We let Karl Malone get it going, and when that happens, he's going to score. Once that happens, it's hard to turn the tide. We turned the ball over a lot and made some horrendous mistakes. But we also made a couple of big plays in the final minute to win.

The big thing as far as I'm concerned is that we won the first two games. We blew some leads in the Seattle series, too, but it seemed to be happening a lot in the playoffs this season; the Lakers blew a lead to Golden State, and Golden State did the same thing right back. I think teams are just so evenly matched that if you don't play up to your capabilities, anybody has the ability to come back on you.

Again, it goes back to the fact that when we get stagnant on offense, we have a hard time turning the momentum back around. But after the game I felt more like dwelling on the first three quarters—which were so good—rather than the last ten minutes of the game.

May 10, 1991

Salt Lake City—We got a break, we feel, from the schedule in this playoff series. After winning the first two games at home, we play the next two games in the Salt Palace. But they are back-to-back games, and that, we believe, is to our advantage.

They are playing their key people—Stockton and the Malones—a lot of minutes. I think somewhere along the line that's going to work in our favor. It may not happen in the Saturday game, but it could happen Sunday, when the back-to-backs take their toll. Plus, they have all the pressure on them to keep pace and win both their home games.

The key thing for us is to play the same kind of game in Salt Lake City that we did in the last game we played there during the regular season. In that game we came out and were smart offensively and moved the ball well. We set the tone. So many times we come here and shoot the ball too quick, and that allows them to get out and run a little more than they normally do. They play with so much more confidence in their own building. They seem to have more to their game at home than on the road.

More people usually get involved in their offense at home than on the road. They open it up a little more and they shoot better at home. I would just like to play a solid game and see what happens. I'd like to stay close and just see.

May 11, 1991

Salt Lake City—We really did play a good game. We just didn't shoot the ball well. We made only 37.8 percent of our shots, and it's hard to win with that kind of shooting—especially when they outrebounded us 56–46.

We dominated them on the boards in the first two games, but they came back and dominated us. They had 17 offensive rebounds. They were much more aggressive than we were, and Karl Malone, even though he shot poorly, had a big game. Mike Brown came in off their bench and hurt us, too.

We were only 3 down at the half and they opened it up to 10 or 11 in the third quarter. It began to look like one of those games where they would just open it up on us, but we came back in the fourth period and made it a game. But we took some quick 3-point attempts down the stretch, missed them, and lost our chance to win. The final score was 107–101.

But you don't feel that bad when you play well and shoot poorly. You know that shooting has a way of evening out. I really don't feel too bad about this game.

May 12, 1991

Salt Lake City—This one, just twenty-four hours after game three, was a battle. We established ourselves on the boards right away, getting 12 of the first 15 rebounds, and played a solid first half, leading 26–22 after the first quarter and 57–44 at the half.

They jumped on us at the start of the third quarter, but we stormed back to take an 82–66 lead with thirty seconds to play in the period. We did everything almost perfectly in the third quarter, but they came right back at us. They took off on a 19–2 surge as we made only 1 of our first 9 shots to open the final quarter.

It led to an incredible final seven minutes of the game, seven minutes that featured an almost unbelievable 18 lead changes. Through it all, Kevin Duckworth was just sensational. He made some huge shots down the stretch, scoring almost every time we got him the ball. He finished with 30 points and 11 rebounds.

It just came down to who would miss first. And they did—first and last. We scored on our final 8 possessions of the game. Clyde made a big jump shot to give us a 102–101 lead, and Utah had the ball with a chance to answer. They had Karl Malone isolated on the left side, and Thurl Bailey made a cut through the lane. Clyde was on him because of a switch, and he beat Clyde on the cut. He was open. But Clyde made one of those plays that only about three guys in our league can make. He made up about three feet in about one second and stole the pass.

They fouled Terry with thirteen seconds to go and he made

two free throws. They were able to get up a couple of 3-point attempts but missed them, and we had a 104—101 win on their floor and a 3—1 lead in the series.

It was a great win for us. They have to beat us three games in a row now. I think they really have doubts at this point. Even though we know they are going to play us tough in game five, we feel good about our situation. You know they'll go down fighting because with Jerry Sloan coaching them they're that kind of team. But we've responded so far like a team on a mission.

And once again it shows you the fine line between winning and losing in our league. Five or six teams can win a championship. What separates the teams that win from the teams that lose? You have to be lucky and you have to make plays. This game reminded me a little bit of the San Antonio series last year. We made some plays and they made some mistakes. We came out the winner and they didn't.

I expect Utah to come out in game five back home and play us tough. But I'm encouraged, too, about the way Duck played. He was 12 for 22 in this game and we need him.

May 14, 1991

Portland—They played a solid game, but we kept Karl Malone under control and off the free-throw line. He got 26 points, but he needed 23 shots from the field to get them, and he shot only 8 free throws. After shooting 53 percent during the season, The Mailman shot only 42.5 percent in this series against Buck Williams.

It was fitting that today it was announced that Buck made the all-defensive team for the second year in a row.

The guy who really lit it up for them in this game was Jeff Malone. He had an outstanding game. I think Utah, if they could add just one more player somehow, is going to be difficult to beat. Other than the first one, all of the games in this series could have gone either way.

Again, we had a nice lead going into the fourth quarter

and had to hang on. But we were confident down the stretch and won 103–96. I think the minutes their key guys had to play wore on them as the series went on. Karl Malone played 46 minutes in this game and Stockton played 45. Jeff Malone played 43. I think when they got down to the end of games, a shot would be missed or a play not made somewhere along the line. So much pressure is on their key people to perform, and that wears on you after a while.

For the most part, thanks to Buck, we were able to play Karl Malone straight up. And the officials allowed him to play Malone as physically as Malone plays. That's the key. Malone is so strong and smart. He's so good at getting position and getting you out of position and beating you up. If you're not allowed to be just as physical in defending him, you don't have a chance. If you're allowed to get into him and do some of the things he does to you, then you have a chance. And Buck is one of the few guys in the league who can do it.

I thought Terry did a good job on Stockton in the series. He was consistent and made John work. He didn't give him many penetrations to the basket. We needed Terry to be an offensive threat in this series and he was; he shot 50 percent from the floor, 92 percent from the line, and averaged 22 points per game. We need him to do that. He wore Stockton down a little, I think.

Clyde didn't shoot the ball well in the series but he got 50 rebounds in five games and averaged 5 assists per game. That's the thing about Clyde—even if he's not scoring, he's going to hurt you someplace else. Because Buck had the matchup he had and Duck had to box his guy out, keeping Eaton away from the basket, Clyde had to pick it up for us and he did. Ten rebounds a game is pretty good for a guard.

It was a solid series for us. Two more to go.

Lakers

May 17, 1991

Portland—I feel good going into the conference finals against the Lakers, who eliminated the Warriors in five games.

I think the Utah series was good for us; the games against the Lakers are going to be similar. I don't think the Lakers want to run with us. They're going to try to keep the score between 90 and 100.

Playing the Lakers in Portland is unlike playing any other team. They've been on top of the Western Conference for so long. For our fans, it's as if they're our final exam. We won the West last season but we didn't beat the Lakers, who lost to Phoenix, so some people still question us. Look, it wasn't our fault they didn't make it to the conference finals. They got beat. They didn't deserve to be there.

I find it amusing this year that everyone talks about them as if they're some kind of surprise team. They won 63 games last year—same as we won this year. They just happened to play a very hot Phoenix team in the playoffs and got beat. And then all they did was go out and add Terry Teagle and Sam Perkins to their team. To have all those people returning and then say they're a surprise in the Western Conference is ridiculous.

It's going to be a heck of a battle. People here get so excited about playing the Lakers—particularly when they think we have a chance to win. But I don't see them as any kind of test. I feel we've passed that stage as a team. We've played them and beaten them; we won the season series and the division.

The town, as usual, is crazy, and the media is full of Blazer stories. *The Oregonian* has stories in virtually every section of the paper about the team. It seems as if everyone is into Blazer mania.

May 18, 1991

Portland—It's the middle of the night and I've already looked at the tape of this game several times. And looking back on it now, I can see a lot of things I would have liked to have done differently. It's all those little things I talked about earlier.

I know what I'm going to read in the papers tomorrow and I know what everybody is going to be saying, because they said it with their questions after the game: my substitutions at the start of the fourth quarter cost us the game.

First of all, the media crush for this game was unbelievable. Us playing the Lakers in the conference finals is like us being in the championship finals. There are so many people and there is so much hype. Every TV station in town has hired a former player to do analysis of the game, and the newspapers are using many more people than usual to cover them. Everything is certain to be overanalyzed. A lot of people are around who have never seen us play and don't know anything about our team.

Anyway, we had good control of the game for three quarters, in spite of the fact that Terry Porter was in foul trouble almost from the first minute of play. That hardly ever happens because Terry just doesn't get called for many fouls. Two that they called on him early in the game were so minor that I couldn't believe they were whistled. People can say that's sour grapes, but it's a fact. They were fouls that had no effect on the play and shouldn't have been called.

Terry had four fouls when the fourth quarter opened with us holding a 92–80 lead. But I had to get him out of the game because I couldn't risk him getting a quick foul at the start of the period.

Many people asked me after the game why I made four substitutions for the start of the fourth quarter, and I'm sure they'll write that I did. But it isn't true. Cliff Robinson and Danny Ainge were on the floor at the end of the third quarter when we built that lead. Two subs were on the floor the whole last part of the third quarter.

We opened the fourth quarter with a lineup of Ainge, Robinson, Duckworth, Williams, and Walter Davis. I didn't have a crystal ball with me on the bench. I didn't know we were going to be ineffective at the start of the fourth quarter. But we were.

I believe Clyde when he tells me something. He played so hard at the end of the third quarter, and when he told me he needed a blow, I took him out. I had to rest him sometime in the second half and I wanted him fresh at the end of the game. I think giving him a rest with a 12-point lead makes a lot more sense than to do it later with a 2-point lead.

Everybody has talked all season long about how great our bench is. Well, if you can't use guys for two or three minutes and ask them to hold a 12-point lead, then our team doesn't belong here.

We got off to a slow start in this game and trailed 27–17 with about three and a half minutes to go in the first quarter. But Danny Ainge and Cliff Robinson gave us a lift off the bench late in the period and we closed to within 33–27 after the period. The Lakers made 14 of their 20 shots in the quarter.

With Mark Bryant, Cliff, and Danny working well together, we took charge right away at the start of the second quarter and had a 62–55 halftime lead. Clyde, Danny, Cliff, and Jerome were already in double figures.

We were up 92–78 before Worthy ended the quarter with a tough jump shot from the left baseline that got them back within 12 going into that fourth period. And then it all fell apart.

A lot of questions after the game were about Walter, as if his presence on the floor at the start of the fourth quarter caused the game to collapse. That wasn't true. The only thing that might have changed is that if Clyde had been in the game, he might have gotten a couple of baskets for us. Or Terry might have. But we weren't stopping them at the other end and that was the real problem. Vlade Divac was backing us in and scoring easy baskets.

The only thing I would do differently now, if I had it to do over again, is leave Jerome in the game and take Duck out at that point. But Duck had scored two or three baskets late in the third quarter to help get us that 12-point lead. I wanted to go with my best inside scorer at the time and force them to defend him inside early in the fourth quarter.

We got the ball to Duckworth twice at the basket. He traveled once and got called for three seconds in the key the other time. We got the ball to Cliff, who had Buck going down the middle for a wide-open lay-up, but he threw it into someone's arms and turned it over. Duck traveled at the free-throw line—which on tape wasn't a travel; he was fouled by Divac, who ran into him and knocked him off balance. We had four opportunities in the first three minutes, and three resulted in turnovers.

But when a team comes back at you as quickly as they did—they ran off 15 straight points, counting the last 2 of the third quarter, and took a 93–92 lead—it's not just what you do on offense. It's what's going on at the defensive end, too. We allowed Divac to back us in four times in a row for 8 points at the start of the quarter. I had Duck out there, and Cliff and Buck—and we still couldn't keep him from doing that.

One thing about coaching, though, is if something doesn't

work, I'll be held accountable for it. If it doesn't work, it's the coach's fault. That's the way it is and you live with that. That's the nature of this business.

Still, we had the game in hand. I think it's pretty obvious in the playoffs that leads are harder to hold on to. Sometimes you keep them and sometimes the other team makes a run at you. But it was never as if we were going to just blow them away.

We were 3 points ahead with three minutes to go in the game and were called for an illegal defense—another call that doesn't hold up on the videotape—and suddenly the game is tied. And we didn't do what we had to do down the stretch. We missed a couple of free throws with 33 seconds to go and we made some mistakes.

They beat us 111–106 to swipe the homecourt advantage away in the series' very first game.

May 19, 1991

Portland—I sat down this afternoon and watched the Bulls and Detroit, and it was kind of funny. At the start of the fourth period Phil Jackson, the Chicago coach, has four substitutes out on the floor with Michael Jordan. They had a 9-point lead. Instead of blowing it, they hiked the lead up to 13 points when the starters came back in.

It was more of a substitution than I made, but his worked. Mine didn't. There are just so many little things.

The Sunday *Oregonian* was full of stuff about the game, including the weekly column that I write—which was written prior to game one—and a guest column by former Blazer center Bill Walton. Walton has been working for KOIN, the local CBS affiliate and the station that carries our games, as a guest analyst through the early rounds, and—playoffs are such an extravaganza in Portland—I guess *The Oregonian* wanted to get in on it with a guest columnist.

When you're coaching the team, you're going to be asked about these things time after time after time. I was asked by a number of people throughout the Seattle and Utah series what I thought of things Walton had said. But I didn't know what he was saying because I never saw him on TV. He was even on the postgame radio show that our club runs, but I don't have a chance to listen to it much and I heard him only one time.

After we beat Utah he made some comments about Mark Eaton that I didn't like. He made a joke of Eaton, saying he wasn't a good player and they could never win with him and that he couldn't do this or that. I thought that was a real cheap shot on his part. Eaton has worked his tail off to play in the league and has become an impact player. He has been defensive player of the year. He's one of the reasons Utah is where they are. He has liabilities and limitations, but so do most players.

I thought it was unfair that he blamed Eaton for Utah's problems. I thought Walton was trying to make a name for himself at someone else's expense.

But I didn't think much more about it until I picked up the paper today and saw a number of comments he made about our team, not only about my substitutions in the fourth quarter but about some of our players. He made some statements about things we were trying to do in the game that were totally inaccurate. But because of who he is, because he once led this franchise to a championship, people take what he says as gospel.

If he's going to become an analyst of basketball, he should be professional about it. He should come talk to the coaches about what they are trying to do. He should at least drop by a practice; he came to one practice all season and spent the whole time reading the newspaper.

That column of his really irked me. I've been doing a weekly column in *The Oregonian* for the last two seasons, and it's one vehicle I can use to get my side of the story out in my own words. I may do that next weekend but I haven't made up my mind yet. A lot of times it's pretty hard to come up with a good column that I think is interesting to people. I'll bet they'll be interested in that one.

That's only a minor problem, though. The big task at hand

is getting ready for game two. This is a new situation for us. We got beat in one of the first two games at home and that hasn't happened to us in the past two seasons. We have two days before the next game, and it's going to be two days of answering questions about why we blew the lead and what happened.

But that's in the past now. It's over. And we can't afford to lose the next game. I believe we will win game two. I think the Lakers came up here looking to get a game from us so I don't expect them to play as tough in the second game as they did in the first. I think they'll relax a little.

May 21, 1991

Portland—We kicked the Lakers' tails on the boards 51–28 and got the series even with a 109–98 win. We didn't play exceptionally well, but we played hard and aggressively.

A lot is being said about the way we're defending the Lakers. I pointed out during the Utah series that it's a lot easier for us to double Karl Malone because you really only have to worry about two other guys on the floor. But with the Lakers and the way they are playing, it's difficult to double-team anybody, including Magic Johnson. We can't leave Byron Scott because he's on fire from the outside. Magic is a threat and Perkins is scoring, too. So is Worthy. They have four guys on the floor at all times who can shoot the ball.

And they're a very intelligent team. But I still think there isn't a big margin for error for them. They have to make every shot from the outside because we should really hurt them on the boards. And I think as the series goes along, we'll get better at defending them. The key is not giving them easy baskets. Every basket they make has to be a tough one. The problem is, the way they play makes it hard for you to lock in your defense and make correct decisions.

It's taking us time to find out what we can and can't do. Buck does a good job on Worthy, pushing him out away from the basket, but we'd rather play Jerome on Worthy if we can. We did that for three quarters of the first game and it was working fine. That was also the matchup when we beat them in Portland in our last regular-season meeting. The reason we've done that is that Sam Perkins has changed his game; he's so much more physical and aggressive offensively than he used to be. I don't want Jerome to play him and get into foul trouble right off the bat—because that's where they would have gone immediately. If Jerome gets into foul trouble right away, we're in trouble. During the course of the game we can change the matchup, but we don't want to do it right from the start.

In this game, Buck got aggressive in leaving Perkins and running at the ball to double-team. The move itself, although it got a lot of play in the newspapers, wasn't that successful. But it did set a tone for our team. It made us more aggressive. That carried over into all parts of our game and we played hard. Clyde finished with 21 points, 10 rebounds, and 5 assists, and we pulled away at the end.

May 22, 1991

Los Angeles—After practice and a media session earlier in the week, I was sitting around our locker room with Kerry Eggers and Dwight Jaynes, our beat reporters with *The Oregonian*, Hank Hersch of *Sports Illustrated*, and although I wasn't even sure who he was at the time, Sheldon Spencer, a writer for *The National*.

The local guys were giving me a little needling about Bill Walton telling me in their newspaper how to coach my team and I responded to it. My mistake is that I didn't think it was an on-the-record session, but I guess the guy from *The National* had his tape recorder running. Out of the blue, several of my remarks made *The National* today and it's got the media all stirred up.

I guess that kind of makes up my mind for me. My Sunday column in *The Oregonian* is going to address the Walton situation. Mary Kay is advising against it. She says I'm just going to give him credibility. She says I can't win.

I'm more concerned with winning a game at Los Angeles. I feel pretty good about our chances; we're having some problems with our defensive rotations, but we'll iron them out. The problem is that if Worthy scores and can shoot over Jerome, we have to try to double-team him. But Jerome, one of our most active defenders, is already on Worthy and so the guy coming to double-team isn't quite as active in the rotation.

We keep talking about getting better in our rotations. But really, we have to get better on offense, too. If we do, I don't think they can guard us. We controlled three quarters of the first game and most of the second game. I don't see any reason we can't still win the series as long as we maintain some offensive consistency.

Critics, certainly, are coming out of the woodwork. Because of the scrutiny this series is getting, everything is being overanalyzed. People are already suggesting that we should make some changes in the way we're playing them.

I don't see why. We should have won the first two games. What we're doing was good enough to win those games so I don't see any reason right now to throw it out the window and do something else.

May 24, 1991

Los Angeles—The way we match up against them was a big topic for debate after this game. But I would challenge anybody who looks at it that way to sit down with me and look at the videotape of what turned out to be a 106–92 loss in The Forum.

Our defensive matchups and our rotations had nothing to do with our losing this game. We were just so poor offensively. At halftime the score was 43–40 for them. We were so bad. We kept trying to penetrate, and of course, that was their game plan—which is the same thing San Antonio did against us in the past. Phoenix has tried it, too. Anybody who has played us a lot knows, and I'm not giving away any secrets, that if you can keep us from getting to the basket, make us an outside-shooting team, you can beat us.

If you make us a quick-shooting, outside-shooting team, if you can make us take shots off the first pass or two, then we aren't going to get to the boards. If we run, our transition offense the way we want to, I don't care who you are—you're not going to keep us from getting the ball back when we miss shots. You look at Clyde, Jerome, and Buck—that's three of the best offensive rebounders at their positions in the league. They're going to get to the boards. Duck will get offensive rebounds and so will Cliff.

After that miserable first half, we stayed close for about five minutes into the third quarter. Then we turned the ball over twice and had a shot blocked, sending them out each time on easy fast breaks. They rattled off 12 points and took the game from 49–47 to 61–47 in about a two-and-a-half-minute span and that just about finished us.

We trailed 70–59 going into the fourth quarter—not an insurmountable margin—but they outscored us 11–2 to open the period and we sunk. A.C. Green hurt us off their bench, getting 9 points and 9 rebounds. Magic had 19 assists. We made only 37 percent of our shots.

Someone told me Pat Riley said our offense can't win. That's not true. We can't win a championship playing the way the Lakers play because we don't have their personnel. I don't have a guy like James Worthy who is going to catch the ball, turn around, and shoot a jump shot right in your face. That's a great offense. You throw the ball to him, he turns around and shoots it right over the top of you. If you don't have people who can do that, you have to manufacture things that are going to put your players in positions that give them the best chance to succeed.

We've proven we can win. We've proven we're good at the end of games. Our problem is not down at the end of the game in halfcourt. Our problems come earlier in the games when we get impatient and try to do it all at once. We try too hard to turn things back in our favor too quickly.

On offense, we have to take our plays a little deeper, to
another option. We need to make our opponent work to
defend us. On defense, we have to be solid and make our
opponents work for a shot. Sometimes, we seem to want
the flow of the game to turn in our favor too quickly. We
have to sense when things are going badly and not com-
pound the problem by getting impatient.

Sometimes it seems so hard for our guys to understand.
We've been winning. We've been successful. But the Lakers
are doing what other teams do against us—playing some
version of a 2-3 zone—and we're not scoring.

The thing the Lakers do better against us than other teams
is that when they miss, they get all five people back on
defense in the paint. So when we make that first pass in our
transition game, there's nothing for us there. We just don't
have anything. They're doing a great job of getting back and
helping each other.

We haven't been making the extra passes we need to get
them moving when they pack the lane. We keep talking
about making three or four passes. We know we have to
space the floor. But in this game, if we had 80 possessions
in transition, 65 times we took the shot off the first one or
two passes.

We have guys who can beat people off the dribble and
get to the basket. Sometimes, though, they have to realize
what's going on defensively. I tried calling more set plays,
but we were so frustrated we weren't even taking time on
those plays. We weren't executing them.

May 25, 1991

Los Angeles—We looked at a lot of videotape and I think
everyone saw what was happening to us offensively. I feel
good going into the fourth game. I think we'll play well.

Mike Dunleavy has done a great job with the Lakers. He
has them believing in each other. That isn't an easy thing to

do. You've got to make A.C. Green and Vlade Divac believe that when one guy is posting up they've got to be active on the other side to occupy their defenders. If you double Magic and he kicks the ball out to someone, there's nobody to rotate to the open man because the defenders are occupied. They've really done a good job with that.

The key for them is to make their outside shots. If they do, they're a tough team to defend. If they don't, we're going to run against them. When we get them in the open court, we're going to hurt them.

Our team is different. We have to have movement. That's to Clyde's advantage, to Jerome's advantage, and even to Duck's advantage. When Duck is making that little 15-footer, guys can't get to him. Duck had a tough shooting night in the third game, going 2 for 14, and he lost some confidence. But as I told him, out of the 12 he missed, I'll take 10 of those shots every game because he's usually going to make 7 of them. That's why we won 63 games.

May 26, 1991

Los Angeles—We just collapsed. In game three we were in the game but didn't shoot well enough. In this game, which we lost 116–95, I thought we would come out and play a game similar to the game four we played at Utah.

We came out okay. We were in pretty good shape after the first six minutes. We were aggressive and we moved the ball. We were getting to the basket.

But then halfway through the first period it was as if the door slammed in our face. I kept calling time-outs and nothing went right.

We were down 9 in the second period and I thought we had a chance to get back in it, but then everybody on our front line got in foul trouble. Buck was on the bench, Jerome was on the bench, Duck was on the bench. Then Cliff got in foul trouble. I had to play Walter Davis on A.C. Green and he was killing us on the boards. We were 20 down at the half, and even then, I'd seen us come from that far behind at halftime.

We did cut it to 13 at the start of the third quarter, but it wasn't to be. I have no explanation for it. I don't think we choked. I think it was a combination of us having a terrible period, being in foul trouble, and then them playing very well. We couldn't stay close enough in that second quarter to keep ourselves in the game. They kept getting more and more confident and we just couldn't stop them in the second half.

We had a couple of playoff games like this last season on the road. But this time we've also lost a home game and now we're down 3–1.

We had hoped in this game to put some pressure on some of the Laker players who haven't been in this kind of situation before. Scott, Magic, and Worthy had been through a lot of things, but Divac and Perkins hadn't. We felt if we could just stay close and put some pressure on them, maybe they wouldn't play at the same level they did in the first three games. We thought we might see some cracks. But the cracks came the other way.

A lot was said prior to the game about my column in this morning's *Oregonian*. All I did was call Walton on a few things. "Bill says that basketball is a simple game, often over-coached and under-taught," I wrote. "What exactly does that mean? There seems to be a contradiction in his statements, and these generalities are an affront to any person who has attempted to coach. I very rarely call anyone out on what they say, but I believe if you are going to be an authority on something, take the time to do some research and back up your ideas with some facts.

"We are in our third playoff series and Bill has covered each one for KOIN, giving the perception to those in Portland that he is knowledgeable about our team. I believe if you are truly going to do the job as a professional, you would try to find out what our team is trying to do. Walton not once has talked to our coaching staff."

That pretty much summed up what I thought of a column that I also called "very confusing and not thought out."

Many people have already gotten on me and said I was too sensitive about what Walton said. His answer to what I said is that it's a free country and he has a right to say what he wants to say. But no one seems to agree that I have that same right.

I'm supposed to talk about the playoffs. How many times can you say the same thing about the playoffs? I try to come up with something a little controversial once in a while, such as our Christmastime scheduling. So just because I'm the coach of the team, I don't have a right to say what I feel? I just commented on what Bill said.

He made some mistakes about what went on in that game and I pointed out the facts. He also intimated that I should have ignored Clyde's request for a blow at the start of the fourth quarter, saying that Jack Ramsay would have ignored it. I'm sorry, but I coached with Jack and I know better.

The disturbing thing about all of this is that no one seems to want to talk about the content of my column, and the fact that I caught Walton in some obvious mistakes. No one has said what I said was wrong. All they say is that I attacked him and that I was wrong to have done that. I guess it's just one more example of the kind of magnification everything undergoes.

Did I cross some kind of line? Did I violate some unwritten rule of journalism? I guess columnists are allowed to criticize coaches and coaches are supposed to take it. But what about coaches who are columnists? Can't we criticize our critics when they haven't done their homework?

I hear Pat Riley said on television today that I was wrong to get involved in it because it created a distraction for my team. The only time it was a distraction for me is when people asked me about it—and I don't have any control over that. It took me about two hours to write the column. Our players didn't have any concern about any of it. It was no distraction to them.

People say I was thin-skinned and that I attacked Walton

in the newspaper and on television. But it was my column. What else was I going to write about? If I didn't write about it or talk about it, everyone would say I was ducking it. I talked about it on the NBC pregame show only because Dick Enberg asked me about it. I just said I wrote a column in answer to a column Bill Walton wrote.

And really, a lot of people misunderstood. I don't hate Bill Walton. He sent me a telegram today explaining to me that he was just trying to do his job. That's okay. I was just giving my side of the story.

I think Bill should be thankful to me because I probably furthered his career. It was all blown way out of proportion. It wasn't that big a deal. But I'll probably be hearing about it for a long, long time.

May 27, 1991

Portland—We are home with our backs up against the wall. People have already asked me, "Are you going to change?"

Yes, we are. What else can we do? And we aren't changing, really, because of any defensive deficiencies in games three and four. We all looked at the tapes and saw the same thing—our problems were on offense.

But I do feel that we have to do something to change, to give the guys the feeling that we're doing something different here. And to make the Lakers feel we're doing something different.

We decided to put Buck on Worthy, Jerome on Divac, and Duck on Perkins. This will allow Jerome to become more involved in our defensive rotations and to get to Byron Scott a little quicker. Jerome will be the double-team guy if we want to double anyone.

We want to be as active as we can in game five. If we're not, we're going to have a long summer.

I think we were embarrassed. And I think the guys know we have to take another step. We do have to change. But if we don't play better on offense than we did in the last two games, it isn't going to matter what we do on defense. We're going to lose.

May 28, 1991

Portland—We played better. We played harder. It was still a very tough game, and we were ahead only 3 at halftime. But even then I felt better about the way we were playing.

We missed about half our lay-ups in the first half. We were getting the ball to the basket but just not converting. We were getting offensive rebounds but were not able to score some of them. But we did get 26 offensive rebounds, all because we were moving offensively.

You could see it on the floor. Guys were consciously trying to move their defenders and space the court a little bit better. It was a different team from what we saw in games three and four. We were good defensively—our changes worked well—and we beat them 95–84.

We shot only 39 percent and won the game. That's a trademark of our team. But if we're standing around a lot, we can't shoot 39 percent and win. Defense and rebounding won us this game and got us back in the series.

Buck told me before the game he didn't want to come out. He said he didn't need any rest. After the first quarter he told me the same thing; I can rest later, he said. Even so, I took Buck out in the second period. We were playing pretty well and I saw a chance to get him a short rest. He really gave me a dirty look. I rested him for about two minutes, then he went the rest of the way.

I may play him all the way in the next game, though. And I'm going to use Terry and Clyde long minutes, too. You get to this point and if you're going to go down, you've got to go down with your key people on the floor.

May 29, 1991

Los Angeles—By not playing well in games three and four, we cut our margin for error down to this one game. We still have to win one game in The Forum, and this is it.

I feel good about the way our team is approaching this game. We're going to keep it close. Anything can happen late in the game, and I still think if we can keep the pressure on them down the stretch, they could crack.

May 30, 1991

Los Angeles—When we got to our locker room in The Forum, it was amazing—there were dozens and dozens of telegrams from people in Portland, wishing us luck and urging us on. Even flowers were being delivered. It was an incredible sight. The guys sat there, as they dressed, reading them. It was nice.

The start of the game was not unlike games three and four at Los Angeles. I was scared to death at the start of the game. The Lakers came out extremely active and were getting up and down the floor. They were all over us and we were impatient on offensive. We were missing good shots, and for a little while, it appeared the floodgates were going to open again.

I was really shocked because I thought we had learned our lesson. We trailed by 11 points after the first quarter— thanks to a desperation 3-pointer by A.C. Green at the horn. I just didn't know at that point what was going to happen. I keep coming back to the little things. We make one little mistake and don't cover A.C.; he gets off a flyer and knocks it down. It really didn't look so good for us going into the second quarter.

But you build off things as a team. You mature. People forget sometimes that we haven't been together as a group all that long. So much was expected of us this year. But in the second quarter I think our team grew up. We were so determined in that period.

There wasn't a lot of complaining to each other. There was a lot of talking back and forth about what we had to do, but it was constructive and we didn't have guys going off on their own as we did in the other two games at Los Angeles. We continued to make the extra pass. We crept back into the game. Even though we had our backs to the wall, we didn't get panicky as we did in those other games. We stayed with what we were trying to do. And at halftime we were behind by only 5 points.

I felt if we could get the game close in the fourth quarter, the pressure would turn around on them. They knew they didn't want to go back to Portland for a game seven. This was their chance and I didn't know how they would react if they saw it slipping away.

We didn't play well in the third period, though. But we were still just 5 points behind going into the final quarter. This was the type of game I expected in games three and four but didn't get.

We fell back by 9 in the fourth quarter before we began our climb. They made some mistakes in the final five minutes that they hadn't made the whole series. They threw the ball away. They had a chance to pretty well ice the game inside the final two minutes; they were 3 points ahead and Worthy tried to swing the ball to Magic and Clyde intercepted and went in for a dunk. Their lead was down to 1.

Then, with a minute to go, Cliff got a hand on one of Magic's passes. By now, we were disrupting them. I could see the doubt in their minds. We tipped Magic's pass and were off on a four-on-one fast break. Jerome passed the ball to Cliff, who was open for a dunk, and Cliff just couldn't catch it. He lost it out of bounds and we lost a chance to go 1 point ahead.

Then they had the ball and we did exactly what we wanted to do. We made a great defensive play at our end. We rotated and got a 24-second violation out of them. We were 1 point down and had the ball back with nine seconds to go.

I've watched the final play several times on tape. Sometimes our concentration is not good and sometimes we get antsy and try to do something without taking the time to do it right. But with this play, and with no time-outs left, we did exactly what we wanted and got a wide-open shot at winning the game.

It was our "2-out" play again. We got the ball inbounds to Terry, who gave it to Clyde. Clyde had enough patience to wait until Terry got to where he wanted. We set the double screen. Clyde knew he was either going to have the penetration to the basket or dish it off to Terry. Clyde made the right play. They closed off his path to the basket and he found Terry, wide open, 17 feet from the basket.

The shot looked good coming out of his hands, but it didn't go in. It was just a hair short. And so were we.

Walking off the floor among the celebrating Lakers and their fans, I felt numb. I had to figure out a way to compose myself before I walked into our locker room. After leaving the floor and entering the tunnel, we had to walk about 100 feet past the Laker locker room, through a crowded hallway filled with media.

I thought of all the effort our team had put forth this season, only to see everything we had worked for slip just beyond our reach. What could I say, knowing their tremendous disappointment? I know one thing I was going to try to do—try not to let them feel like failures, if that was possible.

As I entered the locker room there was silence. I took off my jacket and studied their faces. I remember thinking that they didn't deserve this kind of ending. Everyone executed the last play to perfection. Clyde made the right decision with his pass to Terry; Terry has won so many games for us in this type of situation.

This time he just missed. It happens. You can't put the game on that last shot or that missed fast-break opportunity. Cliff mishandled a pass he probably catches nine out of ten times. It happens. We had plenty of other opportunities before the last play. That's exactly what I told Cliff. I also reminded him it was his deflection of Magic's pass that set up the play.

Too much work, too many sacrifices, too much effort, and too many good things had happened this year to be torn apart by this loss. We will still be a team that will challenge next year. Only a negative response by ourselves or serious injury can tear our team apart. We learned ways to do things better. We didn't play well by our standards during the whole Laker series—and still almost took the series to seven games.

There is room for improvement. We can come back next year and be better. I told them, "Let's handle this defeat like we have everything all year—the right way. Give the Lakers their due."

Our goal now is to be better next year and get the same chance next season. That's what I told them and that's what I believe.

After talking to the team, the media, and the well-wishers, I was truly exhausted. I sat in the locker room and couldn't believe the season was really over. I realized then that I fully expected to win the game and the series. I never doubted our team's ability to do it. I thought to myself that we had twice come so close to winning a championship. I had to do something during the summer and next season to give the team the edge it needs to take the final step.

We have enough to win. We just need that little edge that champions have.

That cold I caught in December never really went away. I haven't been doing my jogging the way I used to. I've gained a little more weight. It's been a long road to June. We fell one day—and one shot—short.

The Summer

July 8, 1991

Portland—I didn't watch much of the Finals on television. I have the games on tape and I'm beginning to look at them a little now.

I've said it often: there's so little difference between winning and losing in our league. Michael Jordan made that shot down the stretch at Los Angeles to tie the game and send it into overtime, and the Bulls just go on and sweep the series from that point. He makes the shot and that's it, the series is over. The Bulls got their homecourt back and it was all over.

There are reasons why we lost our series to the Lakers. But we're still a team that can win a championship. I think we were one shot away from winning it. No, it's not fair to say that. Chicago won it and deserved to win it. They're the best team in the league and you can't argue that point. You can't say we would have beaten Chicago. They proved they deserve to be the champions.

But I think it would have been a great final. We played them well in the regular season. But it doesn't matter; we lost and we didn't get there. I give the Lakers a lot of credit. They didn't have enough left to beat Chicago, but they had injuries. Worthy got hurt in our series and that hurt the Lakers a lot.

But we can't lose sight of what we have. We can win with the twelve players we have on our team right now. We're not talking about a break here or a change there. No. We can win the title with what we have right now. Not a lot of teams can say that.

Someone was startled when I said it would have been a lot worse if we had played really well and lost games three and four. They said, well, you can't feel good about the way you played. No, I don't feel good about the way we played. But that wasn't us. I know we can do better. If we had played well and lost, then we would have to doubt ourselves. Then I would wonder if we were good enough and doubt what we were doing. But we didn't give ourselves a chance. We can't afford next season to have games like games three and four. We have to be more consistent and just better than we were this year. But we're a team that can win.

People say you have to fail before you can succeed. That's one way to put it. I think it's better to say you have to mature before you can succeed. And you can mature in many ways.

We could have been lucky somehow and won when we faced Detroit. We could have been fortunate enough in the Laker series to have Worthy or Scott hurt and not play, as happened for Chicago. That could have gotten us to the Finals again. It's not so much that you have to have failure. I think you just have to have experience. You have to find out what it takes for you to win. Chicago has done that.

A couple of their guys matured. Scottie Pippen made the next step. John Paxson stepped up and had a great series. Bill Cartwright and Horace Grant did solid jobs for them. Cliff Levingston came in and helped. Sometimes it's just a matter of having that confidence and taking advantage of it. We had a lot of guys step up last season. But I saw us have some immature periods in the Laker series. But we're so close, we can take that next step.

And maybe our failure this season will help us do that.

Everyone is all over Duck. Last year everyone was all over Pippen because in the big game during the playoffs against

Detroit he got a migraine headache. But this year he's a key performer for an NBA champion. And who is to say Kevin Duckworth can't come back next year and do the same thing? People forget how well he played against Utah in that game we won in the Salt Palace.

Duck would be the first one to tell you he would have loved to have a better series against the Lakers. He's very frustrated. But there aren't many centers in this league as good as he is. I'm not going to throw out what he's given us and the three years of progress he's made and the two all-star games he's played in, just because he struggled in a few playoff games. People were saying last season that Scottie Pippen wouldn't play in big games, and now he's going to be wearing a ring—and he had a lot to do with the Bulls winning.

For our team, Duck is a great center.

For our town, losing was very, very difficult. I joked earlier, during the Seattle series, about what the suicide rate in Portland would be if we lost. But people here are just so involved. And they look, sometimes, for someone to blame. It could be me for my substitutions in the fourth quarter of the first game of the series, or it could be Duck for not making shots throughout the series.

But the team is just so important to so many people. Since the end of the playoffs, I've received hundreds of cards and letters, and all but two of them have been supportive. Even the two negative ones were only negative toward me, for screwing things up. It wasn't as if they were mad at the team.

A lot of the letters were just kind of "Keep your head up." Or inspirational quotes. Or stories of what the team has done for them. The response has been incredible.

There was so much initial disappointment, but I think for the most part people have stepped back now and said, hey, we have a good team. We have a chance. And I think we have to be cautious in our front office. We have to make sure we don't jump the gun on things. I think there's often a tendency to say you're so close, you have to make a change. But look at the teams that have made the big steps, such as Detroit. They didn't change. They didn't trade anybody. They added people to what they had. Chicago didn't trade any of their key people—they just added. Once in a while you can change, and our changing came with Danny Ainge and Buck.

We have some good young people on our roster and we want to continue to bring them along. We want to keep that balance going between veterans and youth. But it's a fine line. You want to develop players, but you don't want to disrupt what you have that gives you a chance to win just to bring along young players.

We have twelve guys right now whom we could go into next season with and probably have a very good team. If you can change one of your guys and make yourself a better team, you should look into that. But I think most likely we'll have to improve from within. We're going to have to get better with the players we already have.

In the Chicago predraft camp, Geoff Petrie talked to Billy Cunningham about our situation. He told Geoff, you don't make changes now. He said that when they had Julius Erving and those guys in Philadelphia, it took them three years to get to the top. He said, do you have anybody you think choked? No, Geoff said, we don't think so. Billy told him, "You've got to see it through. You're just a shot away, or a play away. And you're still getting better, right? You're so close, why change it?"

I think he's right. But even though we probably won't change personnel, we will change our approach a little.

We're not going to have training camp in Salem next season. We're going to train at Lewis and Clark College in Portland. I don't think we need to be in Salem anymore. We're going to use Lewis and Clark as our practice facility this year, so we may as well train there, too. It's near where many of our players live.

I think we're past the stage where we need to get away to concentrate on the job we're going to do. This camp is going to be a little different from the last two.

We're going to spend more time looking at videotape this year. We're going to be looking at the things we need to do in order to execute better on offense. Our emphasis will be a little different during practice. We want to incorporate some things into our halfcourt game to be more consistent as we go through the season.

We're going to get a little more technical in some of the things we demand of our players. That's a fine line; I don't want to take away their creativity, but I want a little bit more structure that they can grab ahold of. I think we're ready for that. In talking to the players after the season, I heard that from them. We have to learn to be more patient and not try to overpower teams. Sometimes that means outthinking them.

So I'll be doing things differently. We're going to have just six exhibition games, which I prefer. Our schedule lends itself to a good start of the regular season, so if we play well, we'll get off to a good start again.

I will be a little more demanding of the players next season. I've already told some of the players that. We've got to recognize the things that get us into trouble and eliminate the errors or find ways to improve. We have enough versatility that we can hurt people in a lot of ways. We must pay more attention to our execution.

I want us to be a more well-rounded team. I don't want to change the way we play because we're too good at that. But in sections of the game we're inconsistent and have dry periods, and we have to do something about that. We have to be more consistent. John, Jack, and I are going to spend a lot of time this summer looking at tape and coming up with ways to do that.

We need to change a little, but I don't think it's a life-or-death thing for us. I'm not going to make wholesale changes because we had a disappointment. We're just going to fine-tune it.

I didn't enjoy this season as much as I did last year, and I don't think the players did, either. I think we handled it well. I think we were focused enough that we understood what we had to do to succeed, but it wasn't as much fun. In a lot of ways it wasn't even as satisfying, even though we won 63 games. That's natural because our goals were different this year from last year. Last year, after the first round, everything was a plus. This year anything short of a championship was a minus.

There were times, even when we were winning, when we had to answer questions about why we couldn't make free throws or why we blew leads or why we weren't more consistent. There was always something, even when we were winning. This happens when a whole city's focus is on one professional team.

I think now, looking back on it, that I changed during the season. I think with our year it's impossible not to change. I've always said, if you can't enjoy winning in this league, especially the way we were winning, there's something wrong. Well, there was something wrong. I tried to enjoy it, but I guess when you're expected to win, even when you do win, it's not as enjoyable as when you surprise everyone.

One way I responded to the pressures was to draw inward a little more. I basically stopped going out on the road. I just stayed in my room and read. I was tired of going out and answering questions all the time. I just wanted to be by myself. I just wanted to relax. It used to be that I would unwind by going out and relaxing over dinner, and at times I still do. But many times the conversation shifts to basketball, and sometimes you want to get away.

I got to where I looked forward to just ordering room service. My relaxation came from a good book and a quiet evening. Perhaps some television. You never really get away, but you can try.

I didn't feel good physically from December on, and I'm just now starting to feel better.

I think it's all part of the long season. You think about things too much and you don't sleep as you should.

No matter how much you try to protect yourself from the demands, some of it is going to wear on you. But I still think we handled it well. It was our first time and we're going to handle it better the next time around.

The summer has been so busy so far. Throughout the winter, at charity auctions, we often allow them to auction off a round of golf or a lunch with Mary Kay and me. So the summer comes and we have a lot of these to pay off. We still have one dinner from last summer to pay off.

It's like Mary Kay was saying the other day. When somebody calls it always sounds like such a neat idea and it's a good cause. But it all piles up. Nothing prepares you for success or failure for that matter. All these things come with success and no one ever gives you a book to read on how to handle it. For our team it happened very quickly. You just have to learn it. I just hope we continue to have success and get used to all the things that come with it.

We once acquired a veteran player for our team and he was asked about charity work. He said, I'll do one thing. I'll take one charity. He's an experienced guy and he knows how to handle it. His approach makes sense.

But we've come so far so fast. It's nice and exciting and it's fun. But sometimes it's overwhelming. My basketball camp is a great example of that.

We had the camp last week and we had about three hundred kids. We have a camp store, and I thought it would be a good idea to bring some Blazer stuff over. You sell some candy and Cokes, and some Blazer T-shirts. We thought we brought enough stuff over for two weeks, but after one week we have nothing left. The parents came on Friday afternoon and it was incredible. Buck was there, signing autographs. And some of the parents were more excited than the kids.

They were buying T-shirts, biting the tags off, and putting them on, and getting as many autographs as they could. That's the fun part, seeing the excitement the people have here about the Blazers. I want us to hold on to some of that excitement next year. I really enjoyed these weeks at camp. The kids are so much fun. It makes you feel good when you get such great positive feedback on our year.

July 20, 1991

Portland—Tonight was our third annual Slam 'N' Jam, an outdoor extravaganza held in Portland Civic Stadium. In the past, it's featured various musical groups, a comedian or two, and a rookie game, made up of players from our rookie camp. Our front office does a great job on this event.

This year, though, it was set up as an all-star game, featuring players from our team and various other NBA stars. There was music and comedy, followed by the game, which was a benefit for Ramon Ramos—a former star forward out of Puerto Rico, by way of Seton Hall, who suffered serious head injuries in an auto accident while a member of our team in 1988. Paul Allen has guaranteed $100,000 to Ramon's family—what a great gesture.

Because of various scheduling conflicts and all kinds of other problems, it was difficult to attract players from other teams to the game. Gary Payton and Derrick McKey of Seattle and former Blazers Darnell Valentine and Steve Johnson joined our players for the game. There were no other all-star players but we obviously did not need them; our own players were there.

That was plenty good enough for our fans. And on a warm summer evening, 21,100 people showed up at the stadium for the game. It was an incredible crowd, showing up to watch their team play and to help out a good cause—Ramon's future rehabilitation and care. The event raised more than $100,000. Seeing Ramon and his family always makes me feel good. They have accomplished so much. Any disappointment we had has been irrelevent compared to theirs.

Our fans are what makes coaching in Portland so special. The people truly love their team and their players. They live and die with them.

And that makes me one of the luckiest coaches in basketball.